AF530035

VIJAYSHREE R

21 Days to Emotional and Spiritual Detox

Overcome Lust, Anger, Greed, Pride, Envy, and Delusion with the Bhagavad Gita

First published by Shree's Essencia 2025

Copyright © 2025 by Vijayshree R

All rights reserved. No part of this publication may be reproduced, stored or transmitted in any form or by any means, electronic, mechanical, photocopying, recording, scanning, or otherwise without written permission from the publisher. It is illegal to copy this book, post it to a website, or distribute it by any other means without permission.

Vijayshree R asserts the moral right to be identified as the author of this work.

This book shares spiritual principles and practical exercises inspired by the Bhagavad Gita to guide personal, emotional, and spiritual growth. It is intended for educational, inspirational, and self-reflective purposes only.

The stories and characters—such as Aarav, Avantika, Vaidehi, Neel, and Sameer etc—are narrative representations used to illustrate real human experiences observed in workshops conducted by the author. While the characters themselves are symbolic, the situations, challenges, and transformations described are based on actual patterns of human behavior and learning. Any resemblance to other individuals is coincidental.

The images included in this book are for illustrative and educational purposes only and are intended to enhance understanding of the concepts and exercises described. All rights to these images are reserved by the author.

This book provides guidance on emotional and spiritual well-being but is not a substitute for professional medical, psychological, or mental health advice. Readers are encouraged to apply the practices thoughtfully and according to their own circumstances.

First edition

ISBN: 978-93-344-3597-9

This book was professionally typeset on Reedsy.
Find out more at reedsy.com

To every seeker who is willing to look within and face the truths of their own mind and heart.

To the participants of my workshops, whose honesty, vulnerability, and willingness to confront their inner challenges have inspired the practical exercises and insights shared in this book. Your journeys are living proof that self-awareness leads to profound change.

To the eternal wisdom of Lord Krishna, guiding us toward clarity, balance, and self-mastery.

"The mind, if uncontrolled, gives rise to desire, anger, greed, pride, envy, and delusion. Awareness and discipline bring freedom."

— Bhagavad Gita 2.62–63

"Transformation begins not by changing the world outside, but by understanding the world within."

"The journey of self-purification begins with awareness of one's own tendencies."

- Vijayshree Ratanparkhe

Contents

Foreword

The first chapter of the Bhagavad Gita is remarkable: before Arjuna can act, he must **recognize the impurities of his own mind**. Lust, anger, greed, pride, envy, and delusion cloud judgment and disturb peace.

This book brings that ancient insight into a practical, modern context. Based on workshops conducted by Vijayshree Ratanparkhe, it captures real human experiences of confronting inner challenges, transformed into **narrative stories** for accessibility and engagement. Through the story of Aarav and the structured 21-day program, readers can relate to these challenges, recognize them in themselves, and take practical steps to overcome them.

It is a rare blend: **real-life observation, storytelling, and the timeless guidance of the Bhagavad Gita**, all in one journey toward emotional and spiritual detox.

Preface

This book is rooted in the human experience of struggle and transformation. In my workshops, participants confronted the six inner challenges—lust, anger, greed, pride, envy, and delusion—and gradually began to overcome them. Observing their journeys inspired me to translate these insights into a **book that reaches a wider audience**.

To make these lessons more relatable, I have used narrative storytelling with characters. While Aarav, Aarushi, Vaidehi, Neel, and Sameer are symbolic, the situations, struggles, and solutions they encounter are **based on real human patterns observed in workshops**.

The goal is simple: to give readers a structured 21-day journey, combining the **wisdom of the Bhagavad Gita** with practical exercises and reflections, so that they can recognize their own inner challenges and transform them into opportunities for growth and peace.

Prologue

Aarav is a boy like each of us—sometimes joyful, sometimes restless. He faces desires, anger, pride, envy, greed, and attachment. One day, by the river, he meets Acharya, a wise sage who explains that these six inner challenges are the root of suffering and that awareness is the first step toward freedom.

Aarav's story reflects the **real experiences of people in workshops**, distilled into a narrative format to help you connect, observe, and apply the lessons to your own life. Each chapter guides you through reflection, awareness, and action, making the teachings of the Bhagavad Gita **practical and tangible** for your daily life.

Introduction

The Story of Aarav and the Six Inner Challenges

Before we begin your 21-day journey, let's meet Aarav—a young boy whose experiences will help us understand the inner challenges we all face.

Once upon a time, in a small, peaceful village, there lived a boy named **Aarav**. He was kind, energetic, and always eager to help others. But despite his good heart, Aarav often felt troubled. Sometimes he was happy and excited, but other times, he felt angry, sad, or restless—without really knowing why.

One day, while sitting by the river, Aarav met an elderly sage named **Acharya**, known for his wisdom and peaceful presence. Aarav decided to ask him about his feelings.

"Acharya," Aarav said, "I try to be good, but I often feel upset or restless. Sometimes I feel like something is missing, and other times, I get angry or frustrated over small things. Can you help me understand why this happens?"

Acharya smiled gently.

"Aarav, the struggles you feel inside come from six inner challenges that cloud your mind and heart. These challenges affect how you see the world and how you react to it. Let me tell you a story."

The Six Inner Challenges

Acharya began:

"Imagine your heart is like a calm, clear lake. When the lake is peaceful, the water reflects the sky, and everything around it looks beautiful. But sometimes, certain things stir up the water and create waves. These waves cloud the reflection and disturb the lake. In the same way, six challenges stir the peace within you."

1. The Wanting Heart (Lust/Desire)

"The first challenge is when your heart constantly wants more—whether it's toys, praise, or attention. You might believe that only if you get what you want, you will be happy."

Aarav nodded.

"Desire makes us feel incomplete. True happiness comes from being grateful for what we already have."

2. The Storm of Anger

"Next is anger. Sometimes when things don't go your way, you feel upset—like when a friend took your favorite toy without asking. Anger makes the heart heavy, but when you pause, breathe deeply, and calm yourself, peace can return."

3. The Endless Wanting (Greed)

"The third challenge is wanting more, even when you already have enough. Like asking for more candies even though your basket is full. Greed is a thirst that can never be quenched, but when you share with others, you find true joy."

Aarav smiled shyly.

4. The Fear of Losing (Attachment)

"Attachment comes when you love something so much that you fear losing it—like when you worried your little sister might break your favorite toy. But when you let go and share, everyone, including you, can enjoy the moment."

5. The Illusion of Being Better (Pride)

"Pride makes us feel we are better than others. It can make us forget that everyone has their own strengths. True greatness comes from humility and appreciating others."

Aarav hung his head, remembering a time he had laughed at a friend who lost a race.

6. The Green-Eyed Monster (Envy)

"Lastly, there is envy. It happens when you see something someone else has that you want. Envy makes us believe there isn't enough to go around. But when you celebrate others' success, you open yourself to more blessings."

Aarav nodded, realizing the truth in Acharya's words.

Moral of the Story

The inner challenges—desire, anger, greed, attachment, pride, and envy—are the sources of our struggles. By becoming aware of them, we can gradually let go of their hold. When we do, we make space for **peace, love, and joy** to enter our hearts.

Rooted in the Wisdom of the Bhagavad Gita

The lessons Aarav learns from his six inner challenges are grounded in the timeless guidance of the Bhagavad Gita. Lord Krishna teaches that our mind, if uncontrolled, gives rise to desires, anger, greed, pride, envy, and delusion—clouding judgment and disturbing inner peace. By bringing awareness to these tendencies, practicing self-discipline, and cultivating detachment, we gradually purify our mind and heart. This book uses these principles as a practical guide, helping you apply Krishna's wisdom to recognize, understand, and overcome these inner impurities in daily life.

Why This Book is Essential for Transformation and Growth

Are you ready to transform your mind, heart, and life? *21 Days to Emotional and Spiritual Detox* draws on the timeless wisdom of the Bhagavad Gita to guide you in purifying your thoughts, actions, and emotional patterns. This book is designed to help you overcome the six inner impurities—lust, anger, greed, pride, envy, and delusion—and experience lasting personal and spiritual growth.

Why This Book is Needed

1. Recognizing the Impurities Within

We all carry certain impurities, not as flaws, but as invitations for self-growth. Lust, anger, greed, pride, envy, and delusion often shape our decisions, emotions, and relationships. This book helps you identify these patterns, giving you the tools to transform them into virtues like love, humility, and contentment.

2. Awareness Leads to Freedom

Many of us are unaware of how these negative tendencies influence our daily lives. By bringing them into conscious awareness, this book guides you to break free from habits and reactions that no longer serve your higher purpose.

3. Holistic Healing

Through practical exercises, reflections, and daily practices, you'll learn to cultivate inner peace, emotional resilience, and harmony, replacing old patterns with positive, life-affirming behaviors.

4. Transformational Growth

Whether you seek personal development or spiritual growth, this book provides a structured 21-day journey to detach from material desires, transcend ego distractions, and live with clarity, balance, and purpose.

5. Practical Application of Ancient Wisdom

This is not just a spiritual guide—it is a **practical manual** for daily life. Each chapter offers actionable steps to apply the teachings of the Bhagavad Gita, making timeless wisdom accessible and relevant today.

6. Restoration of Balance

By cultivating Sattva (purity and harmony) and reducing the influence of Tamas (inertia) and Rajas (restlessness), you'll achieve mental clarity, emotional stability, and spiritual alignment, creating a more centered and fulfilling life.

Why You Should Read This Book

- **Personal Transformation:** Release old habits, negative thought patterns, and emotional baggage to become a more peaceful, empowered version of yourself.
- **Empowerment Through Knowledge:** Gain practical wisdom from the Bhagavad Gita to take control of your emotions and decisions.
- **Healing and Emotional Resilience:** Overcome anger, insecurity, and other overwhelming emotions through self-compassion and reflection.
- **Improved Relationships:** Purifying your mind and heart enhances empathy, humility, and connection with others.
- **Clarity of Purpose:** Reconnect with your true self and uncover your higher purpose for a life aligned with your values.
- **Lasting Impact:** This 21-day journey is designed to create long-

term change, supporting your personal and spiritual growth well beyond the initial program.

1

The Six Inner Challenges – Understanding Lust, Anger, Greed, Pride, Envy, and Delusion

From Story to Understanding: The Six Inner Challenges in Your Life

Aarav's story reflects the inner challenges we all face—even my own.

During the 21-day workshop, I witnessed participants confronting and gradually overcoming these six impurities—lust, anger, greed, pride, envy, and delusion—experiencing profound personal and spiritual transformation. Guided by Krishna's wisdom, I felt inspired to bring the essence of the workshop into this book. Within these pages, I share what I've learned, along with practical, step-by-step guidance from the Bhagavad Gita, so that you, too, can embark on your own 21-day journey toward emotional and spiritual freedom—and discover the lasting peace, clarity, and balance it can bring.

Recognizing the Challenges Arising from Impurities

The challenges we face in life often arise from deep-seated impurities within us. These impurities—lust, anger, greed, pride, envy, and delusion—can seem like fleeting emotions or habits, but they significantly affect our mental, emotional, and spiritual well-being. Below is a breakdown of how these impurities show up in our daily lives and the challenges they create:

1. Lust (Excessive Desire)

How Problems Arise:

When we're driven by lust or excessive desire for things, people, or experiences, we constantly chase after them, thinking they will bring us happiness or fulfillment. This creates unrealistic expectations and a perpetual feeling of wanting more.

Challenges We Face:

- Feelings of emptiness and frustration when our desires go unmet.
- Anxiety, restlessness, and difficulty finding inner peace as we focus

on fleeting pleasures.

- A constant craving for more, leading to dissatisfaction and lack of contentment.

Diseases or Health Impacts:

- Mental Health Issues: Increased anxiety, depression, and stress from dissatisfaction and unfulfilled desires.
- Physical Health Issues: Chronic stress leading to high blood pressure, heart disease, and digestive issues.

2. Anger (Emotional Reactivity)

How Problems Arise:

Anger usually stems from unmet expectations, feeling disrespected, or having our egos bruised. It clouds our judgment and leads us to act impulsively, often making poor decisions.

Challenges We Face:

- Damaged relationships due to rash decisions and emotional outbursts.
- Lingering guilt and regret after heated exchanges.
- A toxic environment at home or work where anger perpetuates conflict and tension.

Diseases or Health Impacts:

- Mental Health Issues: Chronic anger can lead to depression, anxiety, and mood disorders.

- Physical Health Issues: Increased risk of heart disease, hypertension, weakened immune system, and digestive issues due to constant stress.

3. Greed (Insatiable Desire for More)

How Problems Arise:

Greed arises from feeling that what we have is never enough. Whether it's money, power, or success, we chase after more without appreciating what we already have, leading us to measure our worth by external achievements.

Challenges We Face:

- Burnout, constant dissatisfaction, and anxiety.
- Disconnection from what truly matters—like relationships, well-being, and purpose.
- Unethical behavior, strained relationships, and a sense of never feeling "enough."

Diseases or Health Impacts:

- Mental Health Issues: Chronic anxiety, stress, and burnout.
- Physical Health Issues: Risk of burnout, sleep disorders, heart disease, and metabolic conditions like diabetes.

4. Pride (Ego and Self-Importance)

How Problems Arise:

Pride arises from an inflated sense of self-importance or superiority, making us resistant to feedback or help from others. It stems from a fear of damaging our self-image and can prevent personal growth.

Challenges We Face:

- Isolation, as we struggle to connect with others or seek help.
- Inability to learn from mistakes or accept constructive criticism.
- Arrogance that hinders emotional and spiritual growth, making us appear unapproachable.

Diseases or Health Impacts:

- Mental Health Issues: Feelings of isolation, depression, and alienation.
- Physical Health Issues: High blood pressure, heart disease, and gastrointestinal disorders caused by stress and lack of emotional connection.

5. Envy (Comparing and Resentment)

How Problems Arise:

Envy emerges when we compare ourselves to others, feeling resentment or inadequacy when we see someone else's success, happiness, or possessions. This constant comparison distorts our perception of ourselves.

Challenges We Face:

- Negative self-talk, feeling inferior or not "enough."

- Difficulty appreciating our own progress and journey.
- Emotional instability, as we focus on others rather than finding contentment in our own lives.

Diseases or Health Impacts:

- Mental Health Issues: Depression, anxiety, and low self-esteem due to constant comparison.
- Physical Health Issues: Stress-related illnesses, including headaches, digestive issues, and weakened immune function.

6. Delusion (Confusion or Misguided Beliefs)

How Problems Arise:

Delusion occurs when we hold onto false beliefs or illusions about ourselves or the world. It causes us to chase goals that are misaligned with our true values, leading us away from our real purpose.

Challenges We Face:

- Confusion about our purpose in life, leading to poor decisions.
- Disconnection from what truly matters, causing dissatisfaction and a lack of fulfillment.
- Indecision and lack of clarity about the path forward.

Diseases or Health Impacts:

- Mental Health Issues: Anxiety, depression, and existential crises due to confusion about purpose.
- Physical Health Issues: Chronic stress, fatigue, and psychosomatic

illnesses as a result of feeling disconnected and directionless.

Breaking Free from Impurities

Recognizing these impurities and the challenges they create is the first step toward transformation. By becoming aware of how they show up in our thoughts and actions, we can begin to replace them with virtues like love, humility, contentment, and compassion. This process of purification will help us cultivate peace, clarity, and authenticity in our lives, allowing us to lead a more purposeful and fulfilling life.

Now that we understand these six inner challenges, the next step is to learn how to overcome them through practical daily practices—this is where your 21-day journey begins.

References

1. The Bhagavad Gita. (n.d.). Various translations and commentaries.
2. Lipton, B. H. (2008). *The Biology of Belief: Unleashing the Power of Consciousness, Matter, and Miracles.* Hay House, Inc.
3. Hay, L. L. (1984). *You Can Heal Your Life.* Hay House, Inc.

2

Day 1: Recognizing Lust (Desire and Attachment)

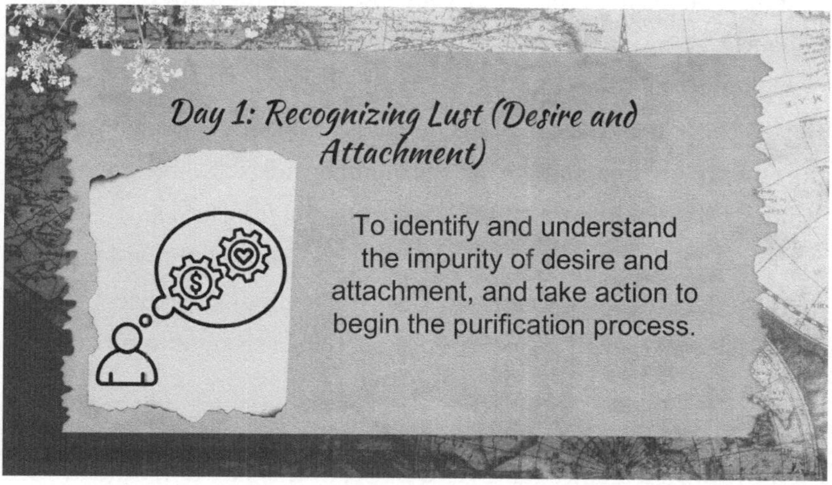

Purpose: To identify and understand the impurity of desire and attachment, and take action to begin the purification process.

Meera and the Silent Dinner

Meera loved spending evenings with her teenage daughter, Anika. They would usually sit together for dinner, sharing stories about their day and laughing over little moments. But recently, Meera noticed something that made her pause. Every few minutes, Anika's eyes would dart to her phone. Messages, notifications, and social media updates constantly tugged at her attention, even in the middle of a conversation.

At first, Meera thought, *"That's just how kids are these days. It's normal."* But one evening, she decided to do something different—she placed her own phone in another room while they had dinner. Almost immediately, she felt the pull to check it. She found herself fidgeting, glancing toward the other room, imagining what she might be missing. And in that quiet moment, a thought struck her: *I'm no different from Anika.*

She realized how often she, too, reached for her phone when she felt bored, restless, or lonely. It wasn't just about the device—it was about a deeper craving to feel connected, to feel seen, or to fill an inner emptiness.

That night, Meera reflected on her habits. She noticed how attachments often sneak into our lives quietly, in ways we don't always see. They don't have to be dramatic or obvious—they can appear as small cravings, repeated habits, or subtle needs for validation. And she understood something powerful: the first step to freedom isn't about removing the object or habit entirely. It's about noticing it, shining light on it, and becoming aware of the ways it influences our thoughts and actions.

Meera smiled to herself. She knew that by simply becoming aware of her attachments, she could begin the journey toward more peace, clarity, and control in her life.

Like Meera, many of us don't realize how much our attachments—whether to people, habits, or material things—quietly shape our thoughts, emotions, and decisions. Today, we begin by shining a light on these hidden attachments and learning to notice them without judgment.

Now, let's use Meera's realization as a guide to explore our own attachments and begin today's practice.

1. Understand the Concept of Lust (Desire and Attachment)

Action: Lust is not only related to physical attraction but also any strong attachment or craving for things, people, experiences, or outcomes.

- **Simple Explanation:** Lust = When you feel overly attached or crave something so much that it impacts your thoughts, decisions, and actions. It leads to dissatisfaction and dependence.
- **Example:** A person might constantly seek validation from social media likes, feeling incomplete without that attention.

2. Recognize Your Own Attachments

Action: Spend 5–10 minutes thinking about areas where you feel strong attachment.

- **Ask yourself:**
- What do I feel like I can't live without?
- What emotions or material things do I often crave or desire?
- **Write down** 3 things or people you feel attached to.

- **Example:** "I am attached to checking my phone for messages, seeking validation from others, and my favorite coffee drink."

3. Observe Your Thoughts and Actions for the Day

Action: For the next 12 hours, pay attention to your mind and actions:

- Notice if you have thoughts or cravings related to those 3 things you wrote down.
- **Example:** "I found myself reaching for my phone every time I felt bored or anxious, hoping for a message."
- Note if these cravings lead to impulsive actions (buying something, calling someone, etc.).
- **Example:** "When I felt stressed, I automatically thought about buying my favorite snack to calm down, even though I wasn't really hungry."

4. Set an Intention to Let Go of Attachment for Today

Action: Pick one attachment from your list and decide not to act on it today.

- For example:
- If you feel the need to check your phone constantly for validation, choose not to check it for the next 6 hours.
- If you're craving a specific food, decide to skip it today.
- **Example:** "I will not check my phone for the next 6 hours to break the attachment to needing constant validation."

Focus on not feeding that desire. You're practicing letting go of the attachment.

5. Evening Reflection (Journaling)

Action: Before ending your day, write down your experience.

- **How did it feel to let go of that desire?**
- Example: "I felt a little uneasy at first, especially when I saw the food I craved. But by not acting on it, I noticed a sense of strength and control in myself. It wasn't easy, but it felt good."
- **Did you feel any discomfort or freedom?**
- Example: "I felt discomfort in the beginning, but as the day went on, I felt more peaceful. It was as if the need to have that thing started to fade away."
- **Were you able to see how much you were attached to it?**
- Example: "I realized that I often turn to my phone for a sense of validation and control. The need to constantly check it became clear to me."
- **What did you learn about yourself and your desires?**
- Example: "I learned that I can feel attached to things without even realizing it. When I stopped acting on those attachments, I felt more grounded and in control."
- **Do you feel any shift in your mindset?**
- Example: "Yes, I feel less reliant on external things for happiness. I see now that letting go can bring more peace than trying to fulfill those desires."

Guided by Bhagavad Gita Wisdom

Lust, or intense desire, is rooted in attachment to worldly things, which clouds our judgment and peace. As Lord Krishna explains:

> *"While contemplating the objects of the senses, one develops*

attachment to them. From attachment, lust develops, and from lust anger arises.

From anger comes delusion, from delusion the loss of memory, from loss of memory the destruction of intelligence, and from the destruction of intelligence one perishes."

(Bhagavad Gita 2.62–63)

Relevance

By recognizing our attachments, we can begin to release the grip of desire, leading us toward freedom and spiritual growth. Understanding the impact of desire is key to self-purification.

End of Day 1

Summary:

- We have taken a practical step in recognizing and detaching from lust/attachment.
- This is our first experience of purification—acknowledging the attachment and consciously letting it go for the day.

3

Day 2: Understanding Anger (Born of Unfulfilled Desires)

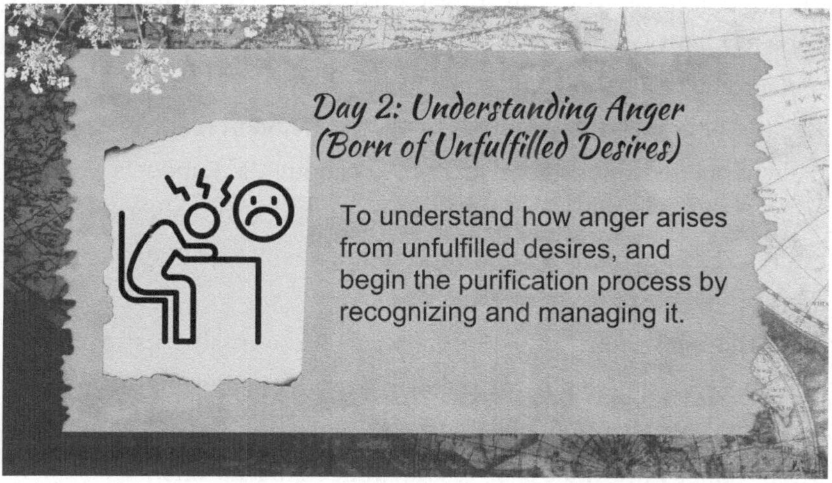

Purpose: To understand how anger arises from unfulfilled desires, and begin the purification process by recognizing and managing it.

Rohan's Mirror of Anger

Rohan had been working on an important project for weeks. He stayed late, double-checked every detail, and made sure his presentation was flawless. The next morning, during the team meeting, his manager, Ms. Kapoor, quickly glanced at his slides and gave a brief, neutral comment. No praise. No acknowledgment of his hard work.

Rohan felt a sudden surge of irritation. His chest tightened, his thoughts raced, and he found himself clenching his fists under the table. For a moment, all his excitement and pride in the project evaporated, replaced by frustration and anger.

Later, while reflecting quietly at his desk, Rohan realized what had truly happened. His anger wasn't really about Ms. Kapoor's words or tone. Deep down, he had hoped for recognition, for validation of the effort he had put in. When that expectation wasn't met, a spark of anger arose.

He thought about other moments in life—small frustrations in meetings, disagreements with colleagues, or even personal encounters with friends—where anger had surfaced. He recognized a pattern: anger often signals unfulfilled desires and unmet expectations.

Rohan also noticed that anger isn't inherently "bad." It is like a mirror, showing us where our attachments, expectations, and desires lie. By observing it carefully, he could understand himself better and respond more mindfully next time.

Like Rohan, many of us don't realize how unfulfilled desires quietly shape our reactions and emotions. Today, we begin by noticing moments of anger, identifying the underlying desires, and learning to respond with awareness and calmness.

Now, let's use Rohan's reflection as a guide to explore our own experiences of anger and begin today's practice.

1. Understand the Concept of Anger

Action: Anger is a natural emotion that often arises when our desires are unfulfilled. It can manifest when things don't go as we expect or when we don't get what we want.

- **Simple Explanation:** Anger = The emotional response when we feel frustrated, helpless, or when our desires are blocked or unmet.
- **Example:** "I felt angry when my presentation didn't go as planned. I was expecting praise for my hard work, but when the feedback was critical, my desire for recognition wasn't fulfilled."

2. Identify Triggers for Your Anger

Action: Reflect on moments when you've felt angry.

- **Ask yourself:**
- What happened right before I got angry?
- Were my desires or expectations unmet?
- **Write down** 3 situations in the past week where you felt angry.
- **Example:**
- "I was frustrated with my partner when they didn't listen to my opinion."
- "I became angry when I was stuck in traffic and missed an important meeting."
- "I felt irritated when a coworker took credit for my idea."

3. Understand the Root Cause of Your Anger

Action: Reflect on what desire or expectation was not met in each of the situations you listed.

- **Ask yourself:**
- What was I hoping for or expecting in that moment?
- Why did I react with anger when things didn't go my way?
- **Note:** Anger often arises when our attachments to outcomes or expectations are challenged.
- **Example:** "When my partner didn't listen, I was expecting them to acknowledge my feelings and show support. The unmet desire for validation sparked my anger."

4. Observe Your Reactions to Anger

Action: For the next 12 hours, pay attention to any feelings of frustration or anger.

- Notice if you feel angry or irritated during any situation.
- Pause and ask:
- Is this anger arising because something I wanted or expected isn't happening?
- Can I identify the desire that is unfulfilled?
- Write down any moment of anger you experience during the day and reflect on its cause.
- **Example:** "When my coworker took credit for my idea, I noticed the anger was fueled by the unmet expectation that my contributions would be recognized."

5. Set an Intention to Respond with Calmness

Action: Choose one situation from the day where you felt angry and set the intention to respond differently next time.

- Instead of reacting with anger, try to breathe deeply and respond calmly.
- **Example:**
- If you feel anger rising due to someone's behavior or an unmet expectation, practice taking a pause for 5–10 seconds, then choose a calm, non-reactive response.
- "Next time, if I feel anger rising because of criticism, I will take a deep breath and calmly acknowledge the feedback, instead of immediately reacting with frustration."

6. Evening Reflection (Journaling)

Action: Before ending your day, write down your reflections on the day's experiences with anger.

- **How did it feel when you identified the root of your anger?**
- Example: "I realized that most of my anger today was because I had expectations about my colleague's behavior that weren't met. When I understood that, the anger felt more manageable."
- **Were you able to identify unfulfilled desires that led to anger?**
- Example: "I wanted validation for my ideas at work, and when it didn't come, I felt angry and dismissed. Recognizing this helped me detach from that desire."
- **How did your reactions to anger change after becoming aware?**
- Example: "When I paused and reflected before reacting, I noticed I was less impulsive. I felt calmer when I acknowledged the source of my anger."
- **Did you feel any sense of freedom by letting go of anger?**

- Example: "Yes, when I stopped holding onto my anger and accepted that things don't always go my way, I felt lighter and more at peace."
- **What is your takeaway about how unfulfilled desires fuel anger?**
- Example: "I learned that much of my anger comes from unmet desires. If I can address the root cause, I can manage my reactions better and avoid letting anger control me."

Guided by Bhagavad Gita Wisdom

"While contemplating the objects of the senses, one develops attachment to them. From attachment, lust develops, and from lust anger arises.

From anger comes delusion, from delusion the loss of memory, from loss of memory the destruction of intelligence, and from the destruction of intelligence one perishes."

(Bhagavad Gita 2.62–63)

Anger arises when desires are not fulfilled, leading to frustration and emotional instability. Krishna teaches in the Bhagavad Gita (2.63) that unfulfilled desires cloud the intellect, leading to anger. Anger disturbs mental clarity and derails our ability to make wise decisions, blocking our path to spiritual growth.

Relevance

Recognizing anger as a reaction to unfulfilled desires helps us disassociate from it. By practicing self-control and maintaining calmness, we bring peace to the mind and avoid unnecessary conflict.

End of Day 2

Summary:

- Today, we have identified how anger arises from unfulfilled desires and began to detach from those desires.

- We have practiced responding to anger with awareness instead of reaction. This is an important step toward purifying the mind and emotions.

4

Day 3: Identifying Greed (Fear of Lack and Excessive Want)

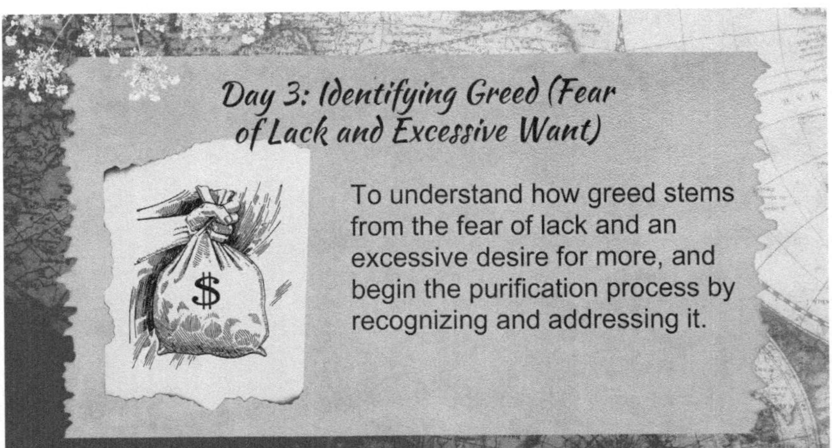

Purpose: To understand how greed stems from the fear of lack and an excessive desire for more, and begin the purification process by recognizing and addressing it.

Vikram and the Unending Wishlist

Vikram had just received his quarterly bonus at work, and he felt a mix of excitement and restlessness. He immediately started imagining all the things he could buy—upgraded gadgets, fancy clothes, and even a new watch he had been eyeing for months. One thought led to another, and soon he had created a long mental wishlist.

During a break, he overheard a colleague talking casually about saving money for a vacation. A flicker of worry ran through him: *"What if my bonus isn't enough? What if I miss out?"* That small fear of not having enough suddenly amplified his desire for more. He noticed how quickly gratitude for what he already had gave way to a compulsion to acquire more.

Later, sitting quietly at his desk, Vikram reflected on his feelings. He realized that greed wasn't simply about wanting things—it was rooted in a fear of scarcity, an inner sense of lack that made him chase more relentlessly. This constant striving left him feeling unsatisfied, even when he had more than enough.

Vikram understood that this fear-driven desire didn't serve him; it only clouded his mind and disturbed his peace. By noticing this pattern, he could start practicing contentment, focusing on sufficiency, and cultivating gratitude for what he already had.

Like Vikram, many of us struggle with excessive wanting, often fueled by the fear of not having enough. Today, we begin by observing these impulses, recognizing where greed arises, and learning to respond with awareness and calmness.

Now, let's use Vikram's reflection as a guide to explore our own experiences of greed and begin today's practice.

1. Understand the Concept of Greed

- **Action:** Greed is a desire for more than what we need, often driven by the fear of not having enough or a sense of insecurity.
- **Explanation:** Greed = A compulsive craving to acquire or accumulate more than necessary, rooted in fear of scarcity.
- **Example:** A person might hoard money or possessions out of fear that they won't have enough in the future.

2. Recognize the Link Between Greed and Fear of Lack

- **Action:** Reflect on moments when you've felt a strong desire for something, even when you didn't need it.
- Ask yourself:
- Did I desire this because I felt I might not have enough?
- Was there any fear behind my desire for more?
- Write down 3 situations in the past week when you felt greed or an excessive desire for something.
- **Example:***"I bought more clothes than I needed because I was worried about not having enough variety, even though I already had plenty."*

3. Identify Areas of Excessive Want

- **Action:** Reflect on areas in your life where you feel you want more than you need.

- Ask yourself:
- Is there an area of my life where I tend to accumulate more than necessary? (e.g., money, possessions, status, food, etc.)
- Write down areas where greed or excessive desire may show up.
- **Example:** *"I feel the need to always buy the latest gadgets, even though my current ones are still functional."*

4. Observe Your Fear of Lack

- **Action:** Notice moments in the day when you feel a fear of not having enough.
- Pay attention to situations where you feel insecure about your resources or future.
- Write down any instance where this fear of lack triggered excessive wanting or greed.
- **Example:** *"I felt anxious about my savings and wanted to buy extra insurance, even though I have enough for now."*

5. Set an Intention to Practice Contentment

- **Action:** For the next 12 hours, practice being mindful of any moment when you feel the urge to acquire more than necessary.
- Pause and ask yourself:
- Do I really need this?
- Am I seeking this out of a fear of lack or insecurity?
- Try to replace this desire with gratitude for what you already have.
- **Example**: If you feel tempted to buy something unnecessary, pause, reflect, and instead focus on the value of what you already own.

6. Evening Reflection (Journaling)

- **Action:** Before ending your day, write down your reflections on the day's experiences with greed. Use these prompts:
- What moments made you feel the urge to acquire more than you need?
- **Example:***"I noticed myself scrolling through online stores, looking at things I didn't need, simply because I felt a sense of emptiness."*
- Did you notice a connection between greed and the fear of lack or insecurity?
- **Example:***"I realized my desire for a new car was tied to my fear of not being able to afford one later in life."*
- Were you able to replace excessive desire with contentment or gratitude?
- **Example:***"When I wanted more clothes, I stopped and reminded myself of how many I already have. I felt content with what I have."*
- How did it feel to let go of greed and focus on sufficiency?
- **Example:***"I felt a sense of relief when I didn't give in to the desire for more. It felt peaceful to be content with enough."*
- What is your takeaway about how greed is connected to fear of lack?
- **Example:***"I learned that greed is often rooted in insecurity, and when I feel secure, I don't feel the need to constantly accumulate more."*

Guided by Bhagavad Gita Wisdom

Greed stems from a sense of internal lack and the fear of not having enough. As Lord Krishna explains:

"The glorious Lord said: Those who are born with demoniac qualities, O son of Pritha, think, 'This entire world has been created for me. There is nothing more than what I desire.' Bound by desires, they indulge in selfish acts and enjoy the fruits of their actions, thinking only of themselves.

Foolishly attached to their own wealth, they become greedy and restless. Their attachment and selfish desires grow, and they are deluded in their actions. Through this, they fall into repeated birth and death in the material world."

(Bhagavad Gita 16.13–15)

Such desires cloud the mind, create suffering, and disturb contentment. By recognizing the root of greed, we can begin to shift our focus toward contentment, gratitude, and the abundance already present in the present moment.

Relevance

Recognizing the root of greed allows us to overcome it by practicing mindfulness, detachment, and contentment. This cultivates inner peace, reduces unnecessary desires, and brings spiritual clarity.

End of Day 3

Summary:

- Today, we have recognized how greed arises from the fear of lack and began the process of purifying this feeling by practicing contentment and gratitude.
- We reflected on moments of excessive desire and started to detach from the mindset of scarcity. This is a key step in the purification process.

5

Day 4: Recognizing Pride (Ego and Superiority Complex)

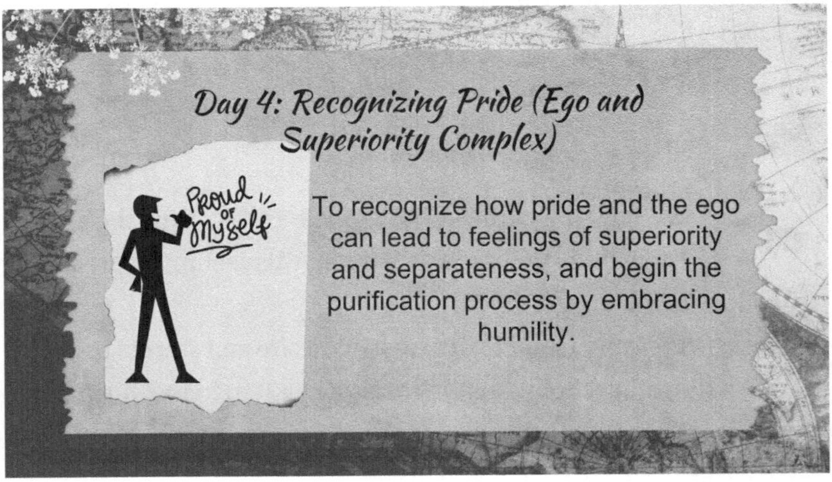

Purpose: To recognize how pride and the ego can lead to feelings of superiority and separateness, and begin the purification process by embracing humility.

Tara's Shadow of Pride

Tara loved teaching art to children at the local community center. She was passionate, creative, and her classes were always full. Over time, she noticed something happening inside herself. Whenever a student painted something beautiful or received praise from parents, Tara felt proud—she thought, *"Of course, they painted well; I'm a great teacher."*

One afternoon, while setting up her class, she overheard two students whispering. *"Ms. Tara is really good at teaching, but I think I could do this better if I tried."* Tara felt a sudden sting. At first, it was irritation. Then she realized it wasn't about the students—it was about her own pride. She had been measuring her worth by her achievements and comparing herself to others.

Later, sitting quietly after class, Tara reflected. She saw how pride had crept in subtly, like a shadow over her heart. Her happiness was often linked to being recognized as the "best," and she felt a quiet need to prove herself better than others. She realized that pride, while it made her feel strong momentarily, also kept her distant from her students, her peers, and even herself.

Tara took a deep breath and thought about how she could respond differently. Next time, instead of letting pride inflate her ego, she could celebrate others' efforts and stay humble. She remembered a teaching she had read in the Bhagavad Gita: true greatness comes not from being better than others, but from humility, awareness, and selfless action.

That evening, Tara journaled about her day. She noted moments when pride had arisen, how it affected her interactions, and how she could practice humility moving forward. She felt lighter and more connected, realizing that letting go of the ego created space for genuine joy and connection.

Like Tara, many of us don't notice how pride and ego quietly influence our thoughts, decisions, and relationships. Today, we begin by shining a light on our own moments of pride, recognizing the underlying ego, and learning to respond with humility.

Now, let's use Tara's reflection as a guide to explore our own experiences of pride and begin today's practice.

1. Understand the Concept of Pride (Ego and Superiority Complex)

- **Action:** Pride arises when we inflate our self-worth, often by comparing ourselves to others. It can lead to a sense of superiority, where we view ourselves as better or more important than others.
- **Simple Explanation:** Pride = When we feel elevated or superior to others, often based on our achievements, knowledge, appearance, or status.
- **Example:** *"I felt proud when I received praise for my work, but the pride made me look down on others who didn't achieve the same. I began to think of myself as more capable and deserving."*

2. Identify Moments When You Feel Proud

- **Action:** Reflect on situations in the past week where you've felt a sense of superiority or pride.
- Ask yourself:
- When have I felt like I was better than others?
- What accomplishments or qualities do I sometimes feel proud of to

the point of arrogance?

- Write down 3 situations in the past week where you felt pride or superiority.
- **Examples:**
- *"I felt proud when my team congratulated me for finishing a project ahead of time."*
- *"When I compared my lifestyle to others, I felt superior for having more material possessions."*
- *"I noticed a sense of pride when I could easily solve a problem that others struggled with."*

3. Recognize the Root Cause of Your Pride

- **Action:** Reflect on what made you feel proud or superior in each of the situations you listed.
- Ask yourself:
- What did I accomplish or possess that made me feel superior?
- Why did I compare myself to others in this way?
- **Note:** Pride is often linked to external validation or a sense of achievement. When we feel that our accomplishments or status make us better, the ego inflates.
- **Example:** *"When I finished the project early, I felt proud because I believed it made me look more efficient and valuable compared to my colleagues. The sense of accomplishment led to feelings of superiority."*

4. Observe Your Reactions to Pride Throughout the Day

- **Action:** For the next 12 hours, pay attention to any moments when you feel a sense of pride, superiority, or ego-driven behavior.

- Notice if you compare yourself to others or feel like you deserve more recognition.
- Pause and ask:
- Is this pride arising from my own accomplishments or a sense of superiority?
- Am I trying to elevate myself by putting others down or feeling better than them?
- Write down any moments of pride you experience during the day and reflect on their cause.
- **Example:** *"When I got praise from my manager today, I noticed a surge of pride. I immediately thought about how much better I was at my job compared to my teammates. I realized this pride was rooted in ego and comparison."*

5. Set an Intention to Respond with Humility

- **Action:** Choose one moment from the day where you felt pride and set the intention to respond with humility next time.
- Instead of letting your ego inflate, practice being humble by acknowledging the contributions of others or recognizing the collective effort.
- **Example:** *"Next time I receive praise, I will acknowledge the team's effort as well and remind myself that there is always room to grow and learn, rather than thinking I am superior."*

6. Evening Reflection (Journaling)

- **Action:** Before ending your day, reflect on your experience with pride and ego. Use these prompts:

- How did it feel when you identified the source of your pride?
- **Example:** *"I realized that much of my pride came from comparing myself to others. When I understood this, it helped me let go of the need to feel superior."*
- Were you able to identify moments when your pride led to arrogance or superiority?
- **Example:** *"I saw how I felt superior when I finished a task quickly. Instead of feeling proud of my speed, I now recognize that everyone has their own pace and journey."*
- How did your reactions to pride change after becoming aware?
- **Example:** *"After recognizing my pride, I chose to remain humble in my interactions. Instead of boasting, I expressed gratitude for the opportunity and the help I received."*
- Did you feel any sense of relief by letting go of your pride?
- **Example:** *"Yes, I felt lighter when I stopped comparing myself to others. It was freeing to recognize that humility is far more powerful than pride."*
- What is your takeaway about how pride and ego affect your relationships with others?
- **Example:** *"I learned that pride creates separation. Humility, on the other hand, brings me closer to others by appreciating their worth and contributions."*

Guided by Bhagavad Gita Wisdom

Pride arises from the ego, where we see ourselves as superior to others. As Lord Krishna explains:

"Humility, modesty, non-violence, tolerance, simplicity, approaching a bona fide spiritual master, cleanliness, steadiness, self-control—these are the qualities of divine beings. Those who possess these qualities attain liberation."

(Bhagavad Gita 16.3)

"Arrogance, pride, harshness, and ignorance are the qualities of demoniac beings. They lead to bondage and suffering, keeping the soul trapped in material existence."

(Bhagavad Gita 16.4, summarized)

"By cultivating humility and avoiding pride, one purifies the mind, softens the ego, and moves toward spiritual growth and liberation."

(Bhagavad Gita 16.18, summarized)

These verses explain that pride and arrogance inflate the ego, create separation from others, and disturb inner peace. Cultivating humility, modesty, and self-awareness helps purify the mind and foster spiritual growth.

Relevance

Acknowledging pride in ourselves allows us to soften the ego and respond with humility. This practice reduces separation, nurtures deeper connections, and supports the purification of the mind and soul.

End of Day 4

Summary:

- Today, you recognized how pride and ego can create a sense of superiority and distance from others.
- You practiced responding with humility and detaching from the ego-driven desire for recognition. This is an important step in purifying your mind and emotions, fostering deeper connections with others.

6

Day 5: Acknowledging Envy (Comparison and Competition)

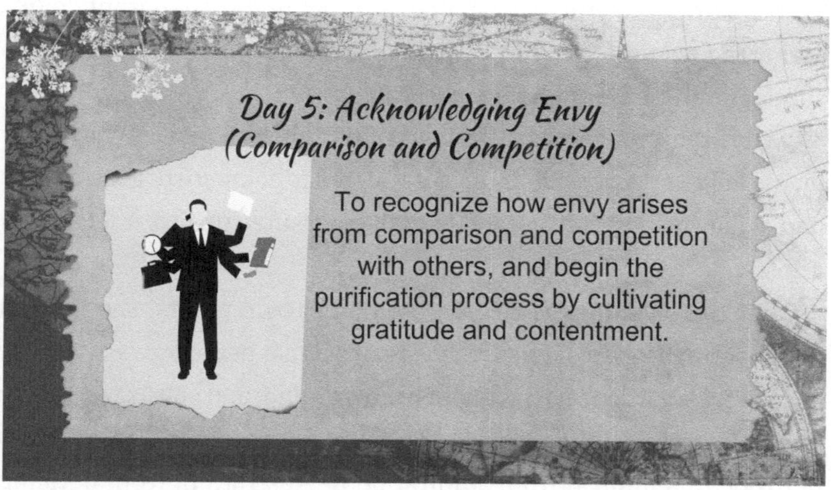

Purpose: To recognize how envy arises from comparison and competition with others, and begin the purification process by cultivating gratitude and contentment.

Nisha and the Garden of Comparisons

Nisha loved her small garden at home. She took care of every plant, watered them daily, and enjoyed watching them grow. She loved the quiet mornings when sunlight would touch the leaves and flowers, and the soft chirping of birds made her feel peaceful.

One weekend, her neighbor, Tara, invited her to see her garden. Tara's garden was full of lush plants, blooming with vibrant colors, and arranged perfectly in neat rows. As Nisha walked through it, a subtle tightness crept into her chest.

"Why aren't my flowers this beautiful?" she thought. "Why do her plants look so perfect?" Her mind wandered to comparisons—what she had, what she didn't have, and how she measured up to Tara's careful efforts.

Later that evening, as Nisha watered her own plants, she noticed the lingering feeling of unease. She realized that her envy wasn't really about Tara's garden—it was about her own mind, and how it had quietly measured her worth against someone else's success. She observed how her thoughts jumped from admiration to frustration, from noticing beauty to comparing and feeling less.

Nisha reflected on other moments in life when envy had shown up—friends getting promotions, classmates receiving praise, neighbors buying something new. She noticed a pattern: whenever she compared herself to others, a subtle dissatisfaction arose. It wasn't anger, exactly, but a quiet restlessness that made her feel unsettled.

Like Nisha, many of us let envy creep in silently, triggered by comparisons with others' success, possessions, or talents. Today, we begin by noticing these feelings, observing when and how they arise, and understanding how they affect our thoughts and emotions. By simply acknowledging them, without judgment or rushing to fix them, we take the first step in the purification process.

Now, let's use Nisha's reflection as a guide to explore our own experiences of envy and begin today's practice.

1. Understand the Concept of Envy (Comparison and Competition)

Action: Envy is a feeling of discontent or resentment caused by someone else's success or possessions. It arises when we compare ourselves to others and feel inferior or deprived.

Simple Explanation: Envy = When we feel unhappy because someone else has something we want, or we compare ourselves unfavorably to others.

Example: "I felt envious when a colleague received a promotion I was hoping for. Instead of celebrating their success, I became frustrated that I wasn't in their position."

2. Identify Situations When You Feel Envy

Action: Reflect on times in the past week when you've felt envious of others.

Ask yourself:

What do I often compare myself to?

In what situations do I feel like I am lacking because of someone else's success?

Write down 3 situations in the past week where you felt envy or resentment.

Example:

"I felt envious when my friend bought a new car and I felt like I could never afford it."

"When a colleague got promoted, I felt resentful because I had been working hard but didn't receive the same recognition."

"I envied a friend's ability to stay focused and productive, while I struggled with distractions and self-doubt."

3. Recognize the Root Cause of Your Envy

Action: Reflect on what was lacking or unfulfilled in each of the situations you listed.

Ask yourself:

What was I hoping for or expecting in this situation?

Why did I feel envious rather than happy for the other person?

Note: Envy often stems from feelings of inadequacy, lack of self-worth, or a desire for external validation.

Example: "When my colleague got promoted, I felt envious because I wanted that recognition too. I realized that I was seeking validation for my own worth through external achievements."

4. Observe Your Feelings of Envy Throughout the Day

Action: For the next 12 hours, pay attention to any feelings of envy, comparison, or competition.

Notice when you compare yourself to others or feel resentful about their success.

Pause and ask:

Is this envy arising from comparison?

Am I measuring my worth by what others have or achieve?

Example: "Today, I felt envious of a classmate who scored higher than me on a test. I realized I was comparing my abilities to theirs, instead of focusing on my own progress."

5. Set an Intention to Cultivate Gratitude and Contentment

Action: Choose one situation from the day where you felt envious and set the intention to respond with gratitude and contentment next time.

Instead of feeling resentful, practice appreciating what you have and celebrating others' success.

Example:

"Next time I feel envious, I will remind myself of my own strengths and be happy for the other person's success. I'll shift my focus to what I am grateful for in my own life."

6. Evening Reflection (Journaling)

Action: Before ending your day, reflect on your experience with envy and comparison.

How did it feel when you identified the source of your envy?

Example: "I realized that much of my envy was rooted in my own feelings of inadequacy. Understanding this made the envy feel less intense."

Were you able to identify moments of comparison that triggered envy?

Example: "I noticed that when I compared my career progress to others, I felt envious. Once I stopped comparing, the envy lessened."

How did your reactions to envy change after becoming aware?

Example: "When I recognized my envy, I took a moment to appreciate what I've achieved and reminded myself that my journey is unique."

Did you feel any sense of freedom by letting go of envy?

Example: "Yes, when I stopped focusing on others, I felt more peaceful and content with my own life. It was freeing to not be constantly measuring myself against others."

What is your takeaway about how comparison fuels envy?

Example: "I learned that comparison only breeds discontent. Focusing on my own growth and practicing gratitude helps me overcome feelings of envy."

Guided by Bhagavad Gita Wisdom

Envy arises from comparing ourselves to others, often driven by jealousy, competition, and desire for what others have. As Lord Krishna explains:

"Those who are envious and mischievous, who are the lowest among men, live in demoniac nature and are bound by the material world. Such people are full of envy and malice, and they are never free from delusion."

(Bhagavad Gita 16.18)

This verse highlights that envy, jealousy, and constant comparison cloud the mind, create delusion, and bind us to suffering. Recognizing these tendencies allows us to cultivate gratitude, contentment, and focus on our own unique path, leading to inner peace and spiritual growth.

Relevance

Acknowledging envy in ourselves helps us break free from unhealthy comparison and competition. By focusing on our own journey and appreciating what we have, we nurture contentment, clarity, and spiritual progress.

End of Day 5

Summary:

- Today, you acknowledged how envy arises from comparison and competition.
- You practiced shifting your focus from others' achievements to your own growth, and cultivated gratitude and contentment. This is an important step in purifying your mind and fostering peace within yourself.

7

Day 6: Understanding Delusion (Misidentification with the Material and Temporary)

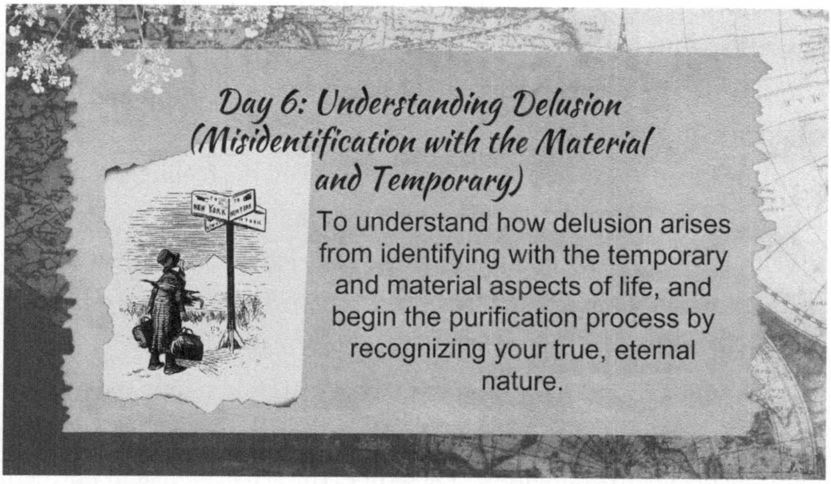

Purpose: To understand how delusion arises from identifying with the temporary and material aspects of life, and begin the purification process by recognizing your true, eternal nature.

The Illusions That Bind Arjun

Arjun had always taken pride in his appearance and his lifestyle. His car was his latest obsession—shiny, new, and a source of pride among friends. Every morning, he would check his reflection in the mirror before leaving for work, making sure everything was perfect. His house, his wardrobe, even the brands he chose—they all felt like markers of his identity.

One afternoon, a sudden change at work shook him. His project was reassigned to someone else, and he realized that his reputation, which he had carefully built, now felt fragile. For the first time, he felt a strange emptiness, a gnawing anxiety that his achievements and possessions could not fill.

Sitting quietly that evening, Arjun reflected on the feeling. He noticed how much he had been identifying with things that were temporary—his car, his job, his social image. These were external and fleeting, yet he had treated them as the measure of his worth. Losing or changing them had created a sense of instability, even fear.

He thought about other moments when this had happened—times when a compliment was missed, a recognition delayed, or a purchase didn't bring lasting happiness. Each time, the sense of disappointment arose from thinking that these material things defined him, instead of seeing them as external objects he could enjoy without attaching his identity to them.

Arjun realized that delusion quietly works this way: it tricks us into mistaking the temporary for the permanent. We identify with things that change, forget that our true self—the soul—is eternal, unchanging, and beyond the material world. Recognizing this doesn't require giving up everything—it begins with noticing how much we tie our sense of self to what is fleeting.

Like Arjun, many of us live in a subtle delusion, believing that appearance, status, or possessions define our value. Today, we begin by observing these attachments, noticing when they influence our thoughts and emotions, and reflecting on the deeper truth of our eternal nature.

Now, let's use Arjun's reflection as a guide to explore our own experiences of delusion and begin today's practice.

1. Understand the Concept of Delusion (Misidentification with the Material)

Action: Delusion occurs when we mistake the temporary, material world for our true, eternal self. We often identify with our possessions, status, or body, forgetting that these are transient and not the essence of who we are.

- **Simple Explanation:** Delusion = When we mistakenly believe that the material and temporary things in life—like money, appearance, or possessions—define us.
- **Example:** "I used to think that my success and the car I drove defined my worth. When I lost my job, I felt lost because I had identified too much with these external factors."

2. Identify Areas Where You May Be Attached to the Temporary

Action: Reflect on areas of your life where you might be identifying too strongly with the material or temporary.

- **Ask yourself:**
- What do I consider most important in my life?
- Do I identify too much with my appearance, job, possessions, or other external factors?
- **Write down 3 areas of your life where you might be attaching too much importance to the temporary or external.**
- **Example:**
- "I often identify myself by my career achievements, and when I don't get recognized, I feel insignificant."
- "I care a lot about how I look and feel anxious when I don't look my best."
- "I've focused too much on my bank balance to feel secure, forgetting that true security comes from within."

3. Recognize How These Attachments Cause Discomfort

Action: Reflect on how your attachment to the material or temporary causes you stress, anxiety, or discomfort.

- **Ask yourself:**
- How does my attachment to these things affect my peace of mind?
- Do I feel anxious or upset when these things are threatened or taken away?
- **Note:** When we identify too strongly with the material, we create a false sense of security. This leads to discomfort and delusion when circumstances change.
- **Example:** "When my job was threatened, I felt like I was losing my identity. My mind raced with thoughts of insecurity because I had connected my worth with my career."

4. Observe Your Attachments and Reactions to the Temporary

Action: For the next 12 hours, observe moments when you attach your identity to temporary aspects of life.

- Notice when you feel stressed, insecure, or overly focused on things that are fleeting (appearance, status, possessions).
- Pause and ask:
- Am I identifying with something temporary right now?
- How does this attachment affect my inner peace?
- **Example:** "Today, I felt anxious about an event I was attending because I was worried about how I would look. I realized I was identifying too much with my appearance instead of who I truly am."

5. Set an Intention to Detach from the Temporary for the Day

Action: Choose one area of attachment from your list and set the intention to detach from it for the day.

- Instead of identifying with the temporary, remind yourself that your true self is eternal and beyond the material.
- **Example:**
- If you're attached to how you look, decide to focus on your inner qualities rather than external appearance today.
- If your identity is too tied to your career, spend today focusing on your spiritual growth or connecting with loved ones instead of work.

6. Evening Reflection (Journaling)

Action: Before ending your day, reflect on your experience of detaching from the temporary.

- **How did it feel when you realized you were identifying with something temporary?**
- Example: "When I realized I was stressed about my appearance, I felt a sense of relief, as I reminded myself that my true self isn't dependent on looks."
- **What reactions or emotions arose when you detached from these external factors?**
- Example: "At first, it felt strange to detach from my work identity, but by the end of the day, I felt more peaceful and connected to my deeper self."
- **Were you able to recognize your true nature beyond the material?**
- Example: "I noticed that when I focused on my spiritual self, I felt more complete and centered, instead of constantly searching for validation outside myself."
- **How did it feel to release the pressure of maintaining your identity based on the temporary?**
- Example: "I felt freer. Letting go of the need to look perfect or perform perfectly in my career brought a sense of inner peace."
- **What is your takeaway about the nature of delusion and attachment?**
- Example: "I learned that by identifying with temporary things, I create a false sense of security. True peace comes from understanding that my essence is beyond the material world."

Guided by Bhagavad Gita Wisdom

Delusion arises when we identify with the temporary material world, forgetting our true nature as eternal souls. As Lord Krishna explains:

"The unreal has no existence; the real never ceases to be. The seers of truth have concluded the same about the nature of the self."

(Bhagavad Gita 2.16)

This verse highlights that the material world is temporary and impermanent, whereas the true self (Atman) is eternal and unchanging. When we misidentify with what is transient, delusion arises, leading to suffering and confusion.

Relevance

Recognizing the impermanence of the material world helps us detach from worldly illusions and connect with our higher, spiritual nature. This awareness fosters inner peace, clarity, and a sense of stability that is not dependent on external circumstances.

End of Day 6

Summary:

- Today, you recognized how delusion arises from misidentifying with the material and temporary aspects of life.
- You practiced detaching from these temporary attachments and reconnecting with your true, eternal nature. This step helps purify the mind by shifting focus from external validation to inner peace.

8

Day 7: Weekly Reflection: Observing the Presence of Impurities

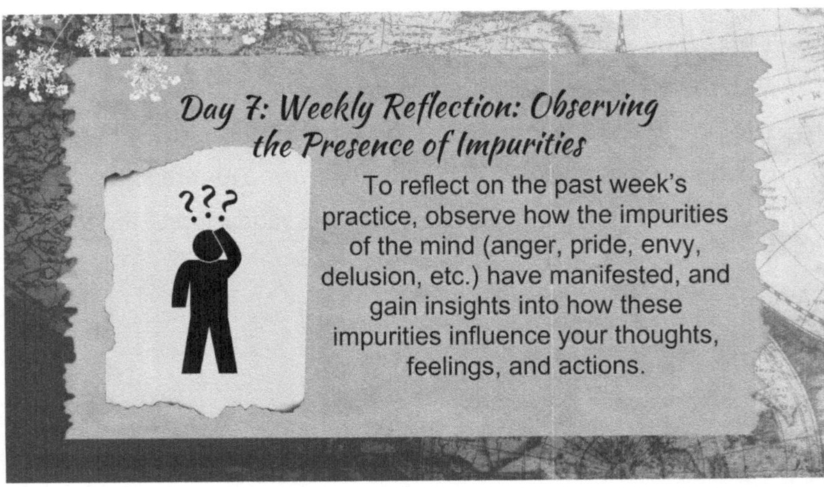

Purpose: To reflect on the past week's practice, observe how the impurities of the mind (anger, pride, envy, delusion, etc.) have manifested, and gain insights into how these impurities influence your thoughts, feelings, and actions.

Priya and the Week of Mirrors

Priya had spent the past week following the daily practices from her workshop. Each day, she noticed small glimpses of her mind's tendencies—anger flaring when things didn't go her way, pride rising when others complimented her, envy sneaking in when comparing herself to friends, and moments of confusion when she focused too much on appearances or possessions.

One quiet Sunday evening, she decided to sit with her journal and review the week. She began with Day 1, remembering how she noticed a sudden urge to check her phone during family dinner, realizing her attachment to being constantly connected. On Day 2, she recalled the irritation that surfaced when her colleague didn't acknowledge her hard work. Day by day, she revisited each moment of pride, envy, or delusion she had observed.

As she wrote, Priya noticed patterns emerging. Anger often appeared when her expectations were unmet. Pride tended to arise when she sought validation or recognition. Envy came when she compared her life to others. And delusion—her sense of self tied to temporary things—showed up whenever she relied on appearances, possessions, or status for security.

She paused and reflected on how these impulses had shaped her interactions. Sometimes, her anger had made conversations tense; pride had created distance in relationships; envy had left her feeling restless; and delusion had made her chase fleeting pleasures rather than true fulfillment.

But as she observed these patterns without judgment, Priya also felt a sense of clarity. By seeing these impurities as reflections of deeper desires and attachments, she realized she had the choice to respond differently. She could pause before reacting, release the need for validation, and remember that her true self was beyond these fleeting impulses.

Priya smiled softly. The week had not been about perfection, but awareness. Each day had held a mirror to her mind, showing her the ways she could grow. Today, she felt empowered to take these insights forward, setting intentions for the coming week with gentleness and patience.

Like Priya, many of us live unaware of the subtle ways our mind's impurities shape our feelings and actions. Today, we pause to reflect, observe, and learn from these mirrors, preparing ourselves to act with greater awareness and clarity in the week ahead.

Now, let's use Priya's reflection as a guide to explore our own experiences of anger, pride, envy, delusion, and other impurities, and set intentions for mindful action in the coming week.

1. Review Your Journey This Week

Action: Take a moment to review each day of the past week and reflect on the impurities you have worked on.

- Ask yourself:
- How have I worked with anger, pride, envy, or delusion over the past week?
- Did I notice any patterns in the way these emotions or tendencies showed up?

Example:

"On Day 2, I realized that my anger often arose from unmet desires at work. On Day 4, I noticed that my pride was triggered by the need for external validation in social settings."

2. Identify How the Impurities Have Manifested in Your Life

Action: Reflect on specific moments when the impurities (anger, pride, envy, delusion) influenced your thoughts, emotions, or behaviors this week.

- Ask yourself:
- Where did I feel the most challenged by these impurities?
- How did these impurities influence my interactions, decisions, or reactions?

Write down examples from the week where you noticed these impurities affecting you.

Example:

- Anger: *"I got angry with a colleague when I felt ignored in a meeting. I realized my expectation for recognition wasn't being met."*
- Pride: *"I felt proud when I received compliments, but when the praise wasn't given, I felt deflated."*
- Envy: *"I felt envious when I saw someone else achieve a goal I was striving for."*
- Delusion: *"I attached too much importance to my social media presence and felt upset when I didn't get as many likes as I expected."*

3. Understand the Impact of These Impurities

Action: Consider how these impurities have affected your peace of mind, relationships, and overall well-being.

- Ask yourself:
- Did these impurities lead to stress, frustration, or confusion?
- How did they affect my interactions with others?

Example:

"When I allowed my pride to take over, I became distant from my friends because I wanted to feel superior. This created tension in my relationships and affected my inner peace."

4. Recognize Patterns and Triggers for These Impurities

Action: Reflect on the triggers or situations that seem to bring out these impurities.

- Ask yourself:
- Are there specific situations, people, or circumstances that tend to trigger my anger, pride, envy, or delusion?
- Can I recognize patterns in how I react when these impurities arise?

Write down at least 3 triggers or patterns you've noticed.

Example:

1. Anger: *"I feel angry when things don't go according to plan, especially when I'm tired or stressed."*
2. Pride: *"I notice my pride surfaces when I'm in a group of people and want to appear more knowledgeable or successful."*
3. Envy: *"I feel envious when I compare my achievements to others, especially on social media."*
4. Delusion: *"I feel confused about my true self when I attach too much importance to external appearances or material success."*

5. Set an Intention for the Coming Week

Action: Based on your reflections, set an intention to continue your purification journey in the coming week.

- Ask yourself:
- How can I handle these impurities more consciously next week?
- What steps can I take to avoid reacting impulsively or letting them control me?

Write down an intention for each impurity you want to address.

Example:

1. Anger: *"Next week, I will pause before reacting when things don't go as planned, taking a few deep breaths to regain composure."*
2. Pride: *"I will focus on humility and recognize the value of others' contributions instead of seeking validation for my own."*
3. Envy: *"I will practice gratitude for my own progress instead of comparing myself to others."*
4. Delusion: *"I will remind myself daily that I am not my possessions or appearance, but my true self is eternal and beyond these material things."*

6. Evening Reflection (Journaling)

Action: Before ending your week, take time to reflect on the progress you've made.

- Ask yourself:
- What did I learn about my mind and emotions this week?
- Example: *"I realized that I tend to react out of anger when my expectations are not met. By observing this, I learned that my emotional*

responses are often driven by desires for control and certainty."

- How have my thoughts and reactions changed?
- Example: *"I noticed that I was able to take a pause before reacting in anger this week, and I chose to respond more calmly in situations where I would have normally felt frustrated."*
- What was my greatest realization or insight this week?
- Example: *"My biggest insight was realizing that much of my anger stems from unfulfilled desires and expectations. This understanding has allowed me to detach from those desires and approach situations with greater equanimity."*

Additional Reflection Prompts:

- How did I feel when I observed the impurities within me?
- Example: *"At first, I felt uncomfortable acknowledging my pride and envy. But as I became more aware of them, I felt more empowered to release those emotions and grow beyond them."*
- Did I notice any improvement in how I handled these emotions?
- Example: *"Yes, I noticed that I responded to situations involving envy with gratitude instead of comparison. I felt calmer and more at peace when I stopped comparing myself to others."*
- What can I do to deepen my awareness of these impurities and purify my mind further?
- Example: *"I plan to meditate more on detachment from the material world and observe how these attachments fuel my pride and envy. I'll also continue to reflect on my triggers to break the cycle of reactive emotions."*

Guided by Bhagavad Gita Wisdom

Krishna advises:

"One should lift oneself by one's own mind, and not degrade oneself; for the mind alone is the friend of the self, and the mind alone is the enemy of the self."

(Bhagavad Gita 6.5)

This verse highlights that self-reflection and self-discipline are essential for overcoming the impurities of the mind. Anger, pride, envy, and delusion arise when we allow the mind to run unchecked. By cultivating awareness, introspection, and a disciplined approach to our thoughts and emotions, we can transform these negative tendencies into tools for growth and purification.

Relevance

Reflecting on our mental and emotional patterns helps us recognize how impurities influence our actions and decisions. By observing and working consciously with these tendencies, we cultivate a disciplined mind that supports inner peace, clarity, and spiritual progress.

End of Day 7

Summary:

- This week, you have reflected on the presence of impurities (anger, pride, envy, delusion) in your mind.
- By observing and identifying these impurities, you've gained deeper insight into how they influence your thoughts and behaviors.
- You've also set clear intentions for how to handle them more consciously in the coming week, helping you purify your mind and align more with your true, spiritual nature.

9

Day 8: Cultivating Selfless Love to Overcome Lust

Purpose: To cultivate selfless love (unconditional love) as the antidote to the impurity of lust, helping to detach from desires and attachments.

Aarav's Gift of Selfless Love

Aarav loved spending weekends with his younger brother, Kunal. They would play cricket in the nearby park, joke around, and share snacks under the afternoon sun. But Aarav had begun to notice a pattern in himself. Often, his joy depended on Kunal following his instructions perfectly or performing in ways that impressed him. He realized he was subtly attached to how Kunal acted and how he looked as a "good older brother". This craving for recognition and control felt small, but it pulled at him, creating tension and restlessness.

One Saturday, Aarav decided to try something different. Instead of focusing on outcomes, he chose to simply enjoy being with Kunal. He cheered genuinely for every hit, every catch, without expecting a "thank you" or looking for praise. His attention was on Kunal's happiness, not his own sense of approval.

At first, it felt strange. Aarav noticed his mind slipping into old patterns—hoping for appreciation, quietly wishing Kunal would follow his tips. But he paused and reminded himself: *"Today, my love is not about what I get back. It's about giving freely."*

As the afternoon went on, Aarav felt a lightness in his chest. The subtle craving for control and validation faded. He realized that his love for Kunal didn't need to depend on outcomes, performance, or recognition. Simply being present, encouraging, and caring for someone else's happiness was enough.

That evening, Aarav reflected quietly. He saw how often attachment to outcomes and desires had shaped his actions, turning love into a kind of transaction. But by practicing selfless love, even in small, everyday moments, he discovered a deeper joy—a happiness that comes from giving, not receiving.

Like Aarav, many of us unknowingly let desire and attachment influence our love. Today, we practice selfless love: noticing when desire creeps in, letting go, and giving freely without expectation. This is the first step toward purifying the heart and overcoming lust in all its forms.

1. Understand the Concept of Selfless Love (Unconditional Love)

- **Action:** Selfless love is love that is not driven by personal desires or expectations. It's a love that seeks the good of others without any attachment to outcomes.
- **Simple Explanation:** Selfless Love = Love without expectation or selfish desire. It's pure, unconditional, and focused on giving without expecting anything in return. This type of love purifies the heart and helps overcome lust, which is rooted in selfish desire.

Example: Imagine loving someone deeply but without any need for them to reciprocate. For instance, when a mother cares for her child, she doesn't expect something in return from the child—her love is given purely, for the child's well-being.

2. Reflect on Lust and Its Impact on Relationships

- **Action:** Think about the impact of lust or desire in your own life and relationships. Ask yourself:
- How have desires or attachments impacted the way I relate to others?
- Do I often expect something in return when I show affection or love?

- **Write down** any thoughts or realizations about how lust (attachment to outcomes, desires, or people) has affected your relationships or sense of self.

Example: I realized that when I show affection, I often expect the other person to give something back, like validation or attention. This expectation creates disappointment when those needs aren't met.

3. Cultivate Selfless Love

- **Action:** For the next 12 hours, practice showing selfless love in your interactions. This means giving without expecting anything in return.

Examples of selfless love:

- Offer a kind word or act of service to someone without expecting appreciation.
- Think of someone you care about and silently wish them well, sending love without needing them to reciprocate.
- Focus on the well-being of others rather than on how they can fulfill your needs or desires.
- **Observe:** Notice any thoughts or feelings that arise when you give without expecting something in return. Do you feel challenged? Does it feel uncomfortable?

Example: I called a friend to check on them, not because I needed something from them, but because I genuinely wanted to see how they were doing. It felt good to give without any expectation.

4. Set an Intention to Cultivate Selfless Love

- **Action:** Set the intention for the day to act out of love rather than desire. When you feel a desire or attachment arising, pause and remind yourself to act selflessly.

Examples of selfless actions:

- If you feel an urge to call someone for validation, instead, just wish them well.
- If you desire something material or personal, shift your focus to helping or serving someone else.

Example: Today, when I felt a strong urge to buy something I wanted, I reminded myself that it's not the thing that will bring happiness. I chose to focus on giving my time to help a neighbor instead.

5. Evening Reflection (Journaling)

- **Action:** Reflect on your experiences of practicing selfless love throughout the day. Write down your thoughts, feelings, and observations.

Questions to guide you:

- How did it feel to act selflessly?
- *Example: At first, it felt strange not expecting anything in return, especially when I gave someone a compliment without waiting for one. But as the day went on, it felt freeing. I felt more peaceful.*
- What were the challenges or discomforts in letting go of desires?
- *Example: The biggest challenge was when I had to refrain from checking my phone for validation. It was uncomfortable at first, but I realized how often I seek that validation.*

- Were you able to act with love without expecting anything in return?
- *Example: Yes, I reached out to a friend just to see how they were doing, without any expectation of getting something back. It felt fulfilling.*
- Did you feel a shift in your emotional state when you chose selfless love over lustful desires?
- *Example: I noticed that when I stopped focusing on my desires and acted with selflessness, I felt lighter and more content. I wasn't as restless.*
- What is your takeaway from today's practice?
- *Example: I learned that true happiness doesn't come from fulfilling desires, but from giving selflessly. The more I let go of my attachments, the more peaceful I feel.*

Guided by Bhagavad Gita Wisdom

Krishna teaches that love, when selfless, transcends desire and attachment. In *Bhagavad Gita* 9.22, He says:

"But those who always worship Me with exclusive devotion, meditating on My transcendental form – to them I carry what they lack, and I preserve what they have."

This shows that when we love selflessly, without expecting anything in return, our heart rises above selfish desires. Selfless love is rooted in seeing the divine essence in everyone. By recognizing this, we can replace lustful desires with pure love and care, acting for the highest good of others, which brings inner peace and spiritual growth.

Relevance

By practicing selfless love, we gradually purify our desires, transforming lust into genuine care and devotion. When we shift our focus from fulfilling personal cravings to giving love freely, we rise above attachment to material pleasures and experience lasting contentment and inner calm.

End of Day 8

Summary:

- Today, you've practiced selfless love as a way to detach from the desires and attachments associated with lust.
- You've taken a step towards purifying the heart by focusing on giving love and care without expecting anything in return.
- Recognizing and letting go of selfish desires creates space for deeper, unconditional love.

10

Day 9: Practicing Forgiveness to Dissolve Anger

Purpose: To practice forgiveness as a means of dissolving anger and healing emotional wounds, fostering peace and inner calm.

Aanya's Quiet Release

Aanya had always enjoyed her morning walks in the neighborhood park. It was her quiet time before work, a moment to breathe and gather her thoughts. But lately, those walks had become tense. Every time she passed by Mr. Sharma's house, she felt a knot of anger in her stomach. Last month, during a neighborhood meeting, Mr. Sharma had spoken harshly about Aanya's volunteer efforts, criticizing her in front of everyone. She felt humiliated, and ever since, she had replayed the scene repeatedly in her mind.

One morning, as she walked past his house, she noticed her familiar surge of irritation. Her chest tightened, and a rush of thoughts ran through her mind: *"How dare he say those things? He doesn't understand the effort I put in!"*

Aanya paused, closed her eyes, and took a deep breath. She remembered something she had read recently: forgiveness is not about condoning someone else's actions—it's about freeing yourself from the weight of anger. She whispered softly to herself: *"I forgive Mr. Sharma. I release my anger and choose peace."*

At first, it felt strange and almost mechanical. The anger didn't vanish immediately. But as she continued her walk, imagining herself letting go of the resentment, she noticed a subtle lightness in her chest. The tight knot of irritation loosened. She realized that the anger had been hurting her more than anyone else.

Later that evening, Aanya reflected quietly in her journal. She wrote down the incident and her feelings, noticing how much holding onto resentment had affected her mood, her sleep, and her sense of calm. She felt a shift—a gentle release of tension. For the first time, she truly understood that forgiveness was a gift she gave herself, not just the person who had wronged her.

Aanya also made a quiet intention: the next time anger arose, whether at Mr. Sharma, a colleague, or even a stranger, she would pause and consciously choose to forgive, freeing herself from the emotional burden rather than holding onto it.

By the end of the day, she felt lighter, calmer, and more present. Forgiveness had opened a space within her heart where peace could grow.

Like Aanya, many of us carry anger and resentment without realizing how much it weighs us down. Today, notice moments where anger surfaces. Take a conscious step to forgive—whether verbally, mentally, or silently—and experience the freedom and peace that comes from releasing emotional burdens.

1. Understand the Concept of Forgiveness

- **Action:** Forgiveness is the conscious choice to release resentment and anger toward someone who has hurt or wronged us. It's not about condoning the wrongdoing but letting go of the emotional burden.
- **Simple Explanation:** Forgiveness = Letting go of anger and resentment, freeing ourselves from the emotional pain caused by others' actions.

Example: Forgiving someone doesn't mean forgetting the hurt, but it's about choosing peace over the constant grip of anger. For instance, when a friend lets you down, forgiving them means you no longer carry that emotional weight, even if they haven't apologized.

2. Identify Situations Where You Hold Resentment

- **Action:** Reflect on recent or past situations where you've felt anger or resentment. Ask yourself:
- Who do I hold anger or resentment toward?
- What situation triggered my anger, and why have I not forgiven yet?
- **Write down** any instances where you're holding onto anger, focusing on the root cause of the resentment.

Example: I've been holding onto resentment toward a colleague who took credit for my idea at work. I haven't forgiven them because I felt wronged and unappreciated.

3. Reflect on the Impact of Holding onto Anger

- **Action:** Consider how holding onto anger and resentment affects your life. Ask yourself:
- How does this anger make me feel physically, emotionally, and mentally?
- Am I holding onto this anger for my own benefit or because I think the other person needs to "pay" for their wrong?
- **Write down** how resentment or unforgiveness has impacted your well-being.

Example: Whenever I think about my colleague, I feel tense and upset. I've noticed my sleep has been affected, and I've been carrying around a sense of frustration and heaviness because of not letting go of this anger.

4. Begin the Practice of Forgiving

- **Action:** Choose one situation where you feel anger or resentment, and begin the process of forgiveness.

Examples:

- Say to yourself: *"I forgive [person's name] for [specific action]. I release the anger and choose peace."*
- **Visualize:** Imagine the person standing in front of you, and mentally offer them forgiveness. You may not feel the emotion right away, but you are making the conscious choice to forgive.
- **Commit to:** Whenever thoughts of anger arise, repeat the affirmation: *"I forgive, and I let go."*

Example: When I thought of my colleague who took credit for my idea, I repeated in my mind: "I forgive them and release my anger. I choose peace instead of resentment." At first, it felt mechanical, but with time, it started to feel more natural.

5. Set an Intention to Forgive Moving Forward

- **Action:** Set the intention to practice forgiveness in future moments when you feel anger or resentment arise.

Examples:

- When someone cuts you off in traffic: Instead of holding onto anger, practice forgiving them immediately and choose peace over irritation.
- In personal relationships: When a friend or family member lets you down, consciously remind yourself to forgive and release resentment, even if they don't apologize.

Example: I set the intention today that when I feel anger rising toward anyone, I will stop and choose to forgive them in that moment. I will remind myself that forgiveness frees me, not just them.

6. Evening Reflection (Journaling)

- **Action:** Reflect on your forgiveness practice throughout the day. Write down your observations, challenges, and insights.

Questions to guide you:

- How did it feel to forgive someone or something today?
- *Example: It was difficult at first, especially with my colleague, but after forgiving, I felt a sense of lightness. I realized that carrying resentment was affecting my peace of mind.*
- What thoughts or feelings arose when you practiced forgiveness?
- *Example: Initially, I felt resistant. I didn't want to let go of the hurt. But as I continued practicing, I noticed a subtle shift—anger didn't feel as strong.*
- Were you able to forgive, even if you didn't feel like it at first?
- *Example: Yes, I chose to forgive, even though I didn't feel it immediately. Over time, it became easier to release the anger.*
- Did you feel a sense of relief or freedom by forgiving?
- *Example: Once I forgave, I felt lighter and more at peace. The anger no longer had power over me.*
- What is your takeaway from today's practice of forgiveness?
- *Example: I learned that forgiveness is not about condoning the wrong, but about freeing myself from the emotional burden. The more I forgive, the more peace I find.*

Guided by Bhagavad Gita Wisdom

Forgiveness is an essential quality that Krishna emphasizes in the *Bhagavad Gita (12.13–14)*. He says:

"One who is free from malice toward others, friendly and compassionate, free from possessiveness and ego, balanced in pleasure and pain, and forgiving, is dear to Me; one who is content, steady in meditation, self-controlled, and firm in determination, with mind and intellect dedicated to Me, is dear to Me."

Anger, which arises from unfulfilled desires, can be dissolved by practicing forgiveness and compassion. Krishna encourages us to transcend anger and cultivate peace, which aligns us with our higher nature and helps us act with wisdom and equanimity.

Relevance

Practicing forgiveness frees us from the bonds of anger, restores peace within ourselves, and allows us to harmonize our relationships, thereby fostering inner growth and tranquility.

End of Day 9

Summary:

- Today, you practiced forgiveness as a powerful tool to dissolve anger and resentment.
- By letting go of past hurts and choosing peace over anger, you've taken a significant step toward emotional healing and inner calm.
- Forgiveness is a key practice for dissolving anger and purifying the heart.

11

Day 10: Embracing Contentment to Counter Greed

Purpose: To cultivate contentment and reduce the influence of greed, fostering a sense of fulfillment in what we already have.

Nisha's Closet of Contentment

Nisha loved fashion. She loved browsing boutiques, admiring sparkling jewelry, and imagining how new outfits would make her feel confident and admired. Every weekend, she found herself scrolling through online stores, adding items to her wishlist—even though her closet was already full, and she had clothes and accessories she rarely wore.

One day, while preparing for a casual lunch with friends, she stood in front of her overflowing closet and paused. She realized she had dozens of outfits she never wore, necklaces that still had their price tags, and shoes she had bought but never even taken out of the box. A thought struck her: *"I have so much already... why do I keep wanting more?"*

That evening, Nisha decided to try something different. Instead of planning to shop online, she laid out her favorite outfits and jewelry. She tried combinations she hadn't worn in months and noticed a sense of joy she had been missing. It wasn't the thrill of acquiring something new, but the appreciation of what she already owned.

The next day, when she felt the urge to check the latest fashion collections, she paused and reminded herself: *"I am content with what I have. My happiness isn't defined by buying more."* Slowly, she felt a shift—her mind was calmer, her heart lighter. The constant restlessness to acquire more began to soften.

By evening, Nisha reflected in her journal. She wrote about the moments she noticed desire arising and how focusing on gratitude for her current possessions changed her experience. She realized that contentment didn't mean giving up enjoyment—it meant truly appreciating what was already hers, creating space for genuine fulfillment rather than endless craving.

Like Nisha, we often feel pulled by the desire for "more"—clothes, gadgets, or experiences—thinking they will make us happy. Today, notice these moments of craving. Pause, reflect, and practice contentment. Appreciate the abundance already present in your life—relationships, health, possessions, and experiences. By doing so, you cultivate lasting peace, gratitude, and fulfillment that no new acquisition can give.

1. Understand the Concept of Greed

- **Action:** Greed arises from an unquenchable desire for more—more possessions, experiences, or recognition—driven by the belief that happiness lies in external accumulation.
- **Simple Explanation:**
- Greed = The desire for more than what is necessary, often driven by the illusion that acquiring more will bring lasting happiness.

Example: I noticed how often I feel restless, wanting the latest phone or new clothes, believing that these things will bring me happiness. But even when I get them, I end up wanting more.

2. Recognize the Desire for More

- **Action:** Reflect on moments when you've felt a strong desire for something beyond your needs.

Ask yourself:

- What was I wanting?
- Why did I feel a need for more, even though I already have enough?

- **Write down** three specific moments from the past week where you felt the pull of greed or an insatiable desire for more.

Examples:

1. *This week, I felt a strong desire to buy a new laptop. I already have one that works perfectly fine, but I thought the new model would make my work more efficient and give me more status.*
2. *I felt a strong urge to buy a new set of clothes, even though my closet is full. I believed that getting new clothes would make me feel better about myself and more attractive.*
3. *When I saw an ad for a vacation package, I thought that if I could just go on a luxurious trip, I would feel relaxed and fulfilled, even though I already have the ability to enjoy smaller, more affordable getaways.*

3. Reflect on the Root Cause of Greed

- **Action:** Consider why you feel this desire for more. Ask yourself:
- Am I trying to fill an emotional or spiritual void?
- Do I believe that having more will bring me lasting happiness or security?
- **Write down** your reflections on what motivates your desire for more and whether it stems from fear, insecurity, or the illusion that more will solve your problems.

Example: I realized that my desire for a new laptop comes from a fear that I'm falling behind technologically. I believe that having the latest gadget will help me feel more capable, but I see now that it's more about insecurity than need.

4. Cultivate Contentment with What You Have

- **Action:** Today, practice contentment by focusing on the things you already possess, whether material or non-material.

Ask yourself:

- What do I already have that brings me joy or fulfillment?
- What aspects of my life are abundant, and how can I appreciate them more fully?
- **Write down** a list of things in your life that bring you contentment, whether relationships, health, nature, talents, or accomplishments.

Example: I have a loving family, good health, and a stable job. These things bring me peace, yet I often overlook them in my quest for more things. Today, I will take time to appreciate these gifts.

5. Set an Intention for Contentment

- **Action:** Choose one desire that you feel is rooted in greed, and replace it with an intention for contentment.

Examples:

- Instead of thinking about what more you need, focus on being grateful for what you already have.
- Tell yourself: *"I am content with what I have, and I am not defined by what I lack."*
- Visualize yourself feeling fulfilled with what is already in your life.

Example: Today, I am choosing to feel content with my current laptop. It serves my needs perfectly, and instead of focusing on the desire for the latest model, I will focus on being grateful for its functionality and the work I can do with it.

6. Evening Reflection (Journaling)

- **Action:** Reflect on your experience of embracing contentment throughout the day. Write down your observations, challenges, and insights.

Questions to guide you:

- How did it feel to acknowledge moments of greed or desire for more?
- *Example: It felt unsettling at first. I was so used to thinking about what I could acquire next that it felt strange to shift focus to what I already have.*
- Were you able to practice contentment with what you have?
- *Example: I felt more at peace when I focused on my family and my health instead of material desires. There was a sense of richness in my life that I had overlooked.*
- What desires did you notice today that stemmed from greed?
- *Example: I noticed my urge to buy new clothes even though my closet is full. I recognized that the desire was more about seeking validation than a real need.*
- How did it feel when you consciously chose contentment over desire?
- *Example: It felt liberating to realize that I don't need anything more to feel complete. I felt a sense of peace that I hadn't felt in a while.*
- What is your takeaway about contentment and how it counters greed?
- *Example: I learned that contentment is a mindset. By focusing on*

appreciating what I have, I can reduce my need for more and feel more fulfilled.

Guided by Bhagavad Gita Wisdom

Contentment is a key virtue taught by Krishna (*Bhagavad Gita* 2.55). He says:

"When a man gives up all desires born of the mind, and is satisfied in the Self alone, he is said to be in pure transcendental consciousness."

When we learn to be content with what we have, we release the grip of greed and cultivate inner satisfaction. Krishna emphasizes that a person who is detached from material desires remains calm and steady, unaffected by the fluctuations of external circumstances.

Relevance

Embracing contentment shifts our focus from material accumulation to spiritual fulfillment, helping us live with peace, gratitude, and an abundance mindset that transcends worldly desires.

End of Day 10

Summary:

- Today, you reflected on how greed arises from a desire for more and began to practice contentment by appreciating what you already have.
- By focusing on gratitude and fulfillment, you took a powerful step in counteracting greed and finding peace in simplicity.

12

Day 11: Practicing Humility to Diminish Pride

Purpose: To understand how pride arises from the ego and cultivate humility to reduce the sense of superiority.

Sameer's Lesson in Humility

Sameer had always been proud of his work performance. At the office, he was known for his quick problem-solving skills, polished presentations, and attention to detail. He liked the recognition it brought—colleagues often sought his advice, and the manager frequently praised his efforts. Inside, Sameer felt a quiet superiority: *"I'm clearly the most capable on this team."*

One Monday, the manager asked the team to collaborate on a complex client proposal. Sameer immediately took the lead, confident that his approach was the best. He started assigning tasks and giving suggestions, almost automatically thinking: *"If they follow my plan, the project will succeed perfectly."*

During the discussion, Raj, a newer colleague, suggested an idea Sameer initially dismissed as impractical. Sameer felt a surge of pride and irritation: *"This is basic; it won't work. I know better."* But before he could respond, he took a deep breath and remembered something he had read recently about humility: true leadership values others' input without the need to assert superiority.

He paused and asked Raj to explain his idea in detail. As Raj shared, Sameer began to see the merit in the approach—an innovative perspective he hadn't considered. Instead of highlighting his own expertise, Sameer encouraged discussion, asked thoughtful questions, and even incorporated parts of Raj's idea into the proposal.

By the end of the day, Sameer reflected quietly at his desk. He realized how often pride had made him impatient and dismissive of others' contributions. Today, by consciously practicing humility—listening, appreciating, and collaborating—he felt more connected, respected, and confident in a healthy, balanced way.

Sameer made a silent intention: whenever pride arises, he would pause, reflect, and respond with humility, understanding that valuing others doesn't diminish his own skills—it enhances teamwork and fosters growth.

Like Sameer, pride can quietly influence how we act in professional settings. Notice moments of superiority, pause, and choose humility. By valuing others' input and contributions, we create better collaboration, inner peace, and authentic respect.

1. Understand the Concept of Pride (Ego and Superiority Complex)

- **Action:** Pride is often born from the ego, where we inflate our self-worth and look down upon others. It's a feeling of superiority that creates separation and blocks our spiritual growth.
- **Simple Explanation:** Pride = A sense of self-importance, where we feel superior to others or better than our circumstances. It leads to arrogance, judgment, and a lack of connection with others.

Example: When I receive compliments, I may feel that I am more capable than others. This sense of superiority can lead to a lack of empathy and judgment toward others, as I place myself above them.

2. Recognize Moments of Pride in Your Life

- **Action:** Reflect on moments when you felt superior or prideful.

Ask yourself:

- When did I feel I was better than others?
- Was there a situation where I looked down on someone or felt a need to show off?
- **Write down** three specific moments from the past week where you noticed pride in your behavior or thoughts.

Examples:

1. *At work, I felt proud of my presentation and started feeling that my colleagues were not as skilled as I am in making a good impression.*
2. *During a conversation with a friend, I couldn't resist boasting about my accomplishments, making sure they knew about my recent achievements in order to gain their admiration.*
3. *I noticed myself looking down on a person who was struggling with their work, thinking I could do a much better job without considering their circumstances.*

3. Practice Humility in Daily Life

- **Action:** Humility can be practiced through self-awareness, gratitude, and by respecting others as equals.

Today, focus on the following practices:

- Speak less about your own accomplishments.
- Actively listen to others and show interest in their experiences.
- Offer a genuine compliment to someone without expecting anything in return.

Example: Today, instead of talking about my recent promotion, I chose to ask my coworker how their week was going and listened attentively to their response.

4. Set an Intention to Respond with Humility

- **Action:** When pride arises, pause and consciously shift to humility.

Next time you feel superior or have a moment of pride, intentionally respond with humility.

- For example: If you feel tempted to boast about a personal achievement, choose to compliment someone else or acknowledge the contributions of others instead.

Example: When I felt the urge to share my recent success with a friend, I decided to listen to their story instead and offered them encouragement for their own efforts.

5. Evening Reflection (Journaling)

- **Action:** Before ending your day, write down your reflections on how you practiced humility. Here are some questions to guide your reflection:
- How did it feel to practice humility today?
- *Example: At first, I felt uncomfortable not talking about my accomplishments, but as the day went on, I felt more connected to others and less focused on proving myself.*
- What moments of pride did you notice in yourself today?
- *Example: I noticed my pride creeping up when I compared myself to others during a meeting. I realized I was trying to appear more knowledgeable.*

- How did you shift from pride to humility in those moments?
- *Example: I stopped myself from speaking and instead focused on listening to my colleague, acknowledging their great ideas.*
- Did you feel any discomfort or freedom in practicing humility?
- *Example: It felt humbling and freeing, knowing that I didn't need to assert my superiority to feel good about myself.*
- What did you learn about yourself today regarding pride and humility?
- *Example: I realized that my pride often stems from insecurity, and that embracing humility makes me feel more grounded and at peace with who I am.*

Guided by Bhagavad Gita Wisdom

Humility is one of the most important qualities for spiritual growth. Krishna speaks of humility as a divine quality that leads to wisdom in the Bhagavad Gita (13.8-12). He says:

"Humility; non-violence; patience; honesty; service to the teacher; purity; steadfastness; self-control; renunciation of material desires; absence of envy; and absence of pride—these are the qualities of one who is wise."

These verses describe humility, non-violence, and tolerance as key virtues that help us transcend pride and recognize the unity in all beings. Humility helps us dissolve ego, see our interconnectedness with all beings, and align with our divine nature.

Relevance

By practicing humility, we learn to release our ego, diminishing pride and connecting with the divine presence in everyone. This fosters unity, compassion, and spiritual growth.

End of Day 11

Summary:

- Today, you focused on identifying moments of pride and practiced shifting toward humility.
- You learned that humility not only reduces ego but also fosters deeper connection and understanding with others.

13

Day 12: Cultivating Compassion to Replace Envy

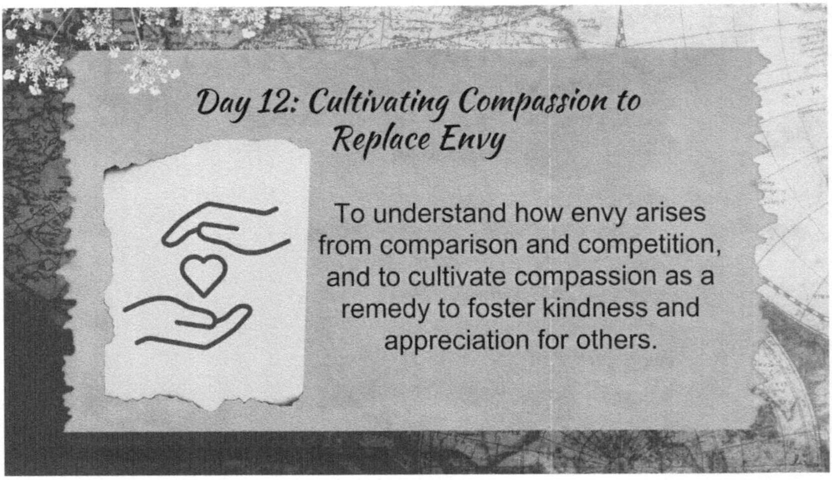

Purpose: To understand how envy arises from comparison and competition, and to cultivate compassion as a remedy to foster kindness and appreciation for others.

Priya and the Light of Appreciation

Priya had always been ambitious and hardworking. She loved her job in marketing and took pride in delivering high-quality campaigns. But lately, she found herself struggling with a feeling she didn't like—envy.

Her colleague, Neha, had just received a promotion Priya had been hoping for. Neha was cheerful, collaborative, and always seemed to attract praise effortlessly. Priya noticed that whenever she saw Neha recognized, a tight knot of jealousy formed in her chest. She would catch herself thinking: *"I worked just as hard. Why isn't it me?"*

One afternoon, Priya was assigned to work alongside Neha on a client presentation. At first, the old feelings surfaced—she wanted to outshine Neha, to prove she deserved the promotion more. But then Priya remembered something she had read about compassion: it wasn't about diminishing her own achievements, but celebrating the success of others while staying true to herself.

Taking a deep breath, Priya consciously shifted her mindset. Instead of competing silently, she complimented Neha: *"I really admire how you handled the client's questions earlier; it gave me new ideas for our presentation."* Neha smiled warmly and thanked her, and as they continued collaborating, Priya noticed something surprising. The envy that had felt heavy and consuming started to lighten. By focusing on appreciation rather than comparison, Priya felt more connected, energized, and even inspired to contribute her own best ideas.

Later that evening, Priya reflected in her journal. She realized that envy had stemmed from her own insecurities and the habit of comparing herself to others. By consciously practicing compassion, she had not only eased her resentment but also strengthened her professional relationships and her sense of inner peace.

Priya made a quiet intention: whenever envy arises—at work, in friendships, or in daily life—she would pause, acknowledge her feelings, and consciously replace them with appreciation and kindness. She understood that celebrating others' successes didn't take away her own worth; it expanded her heart and fostered harmony.

By the end of the day, Priya felt lighter, more joyful, and more at peace. Compassion had transformed her envy into a powerful tool for connection, growth, and fulfillment.

Like Priya, we often feel envy when comparing ourselves to others. Today, notice those moments, pause, and consciously choose compassion. Celebrate others' successes and appreciate their efforts—this practice not only frees your heart but cultivates deeper relationships and inner joy.

1. Understand the Concept of Envy (Comparison and Competition)

- **Action:** Envy arises when we compare ourselves to others and feel a sense of inadequacy or resentment for their success or possessions. It often stems from a sense of lack or a desire to have what others have.
- **Simple Explanation:** Envy = The feeling of jealousy or resentment when we perceive others as having something we lack, whether it's success, wealth, love, or recognition.

Example: When a friend gets promoted at work, I feel envious because I've been working hard but haven't received the same recognition. This jealousy creates a sense of frustration and a belief that I deserve the same success.

2. Recognize Moments of Envy in Your Life

- **Action:** Reflect on moments when you felt envy or jealousy toward others.

Ask yourself:

- When did I compare myself to others and feel resentment or inadequacy?
- What specific achievement or quality in another person made me feel envious?
- **Write down** three specific moments from the past week where you felt envious.

Examples:

1. *I felt envious when a colleague got a promotion I thought I deserved, and I started comparing my performance to theirs, feeling resentful.*
2. *I was envious of a friend's perfect vacation photos on social media, wishing I could afford the same luxurious trips.*
3. *When I saw a family member receiving praise for their achievements, I felt jealous because I believed I had worked just as hard but wasn't acknowledged in the same way.*

3. Cultivate Compassion for Others

- **Action:** Instead of focusing on your own lack or comparing yourself to others, practice cultivating compassion for those you feel envious of.

Today, focus on these practices:

- Celebrate the success of others and be genuinely happy for them.
- Offer kind words or encouragement to someone you admire.
- Reflect on the qualities in others that inspire you, rather than focusing on what you don't have.

Example: When I felt envious of a friend's new car, I chose to express genuine happiness for them, congratulating them on their success and feeling joy for their achievement.

4. Set an Intention to Respond with Compassion

- **Action:** When you feel envy rising, pause and consciously choose to replace that emotion with compassion.
- For example: If you start feeling envious of a colleague's success, consciously remind yourself that their success doesn't diminish your worth. Offer them genuine congratulations or take a moment to appreciate their efforts.
- Recognize that compassion and appreciation for others can uplift both you and the people around you.

Example: During a team meeting, when a colleague presented an idea I thought was better than mine, I consciously chose to appreciate their creativity and contributed my own thoughts with a spirit of collaboration, instead of feeling threatened.

5. Evening Reflection (Journaling)

- **Action:** Before ending your day, write down your reflections on how you practiced compassion and how it affected your feelings of envy.

Here are some questions to guide your reflection:

- How did it feel to practice compassion today?
- *Example: It felt uplifting and freeing to be genuinely happy for others, especially when I congratulated a friend on their success instead of feeling jealous.*
- What moments of envy did you notice in yourself today?
- *Example: I felt envious when a colleague received praise for a project I had worked on, and I realized I was comparing their success to my own.*
- How did you shift from envy to compassion in those moments?
- *Example: I shifted by acknowledging their hard work and sending a message of congratulations, which helped me feel more connected and less resentful.*
- Did you feel any discomfort or freedom in practicing compassion?
- *Example: At first, I felt uncomfortable because I wanted to feel validated, but as I focused on their success, I felt lighter and more peaceful.*
- What did you learn about yourself today regarding envy and compassion?
- *Example: I learned that envy often comes from my own insecurities, but practicing compassion helps me to let go of comparison and fosters a sense of unity with others.*

Guided by Bhagavad Gita Wisdom

Krishna teaches that compassion is essential for spiritual growth. In the Bhagavad Gita (5.18), He says:

"The humble sages, by virtue of true knowledge, see with equal vision a learned and gentle brahmana, a cow, an elephant, a dog, and a dog-eater (outcaste)."

Krishna states that the wise see all beings equally, and recognize the divine essence in everyone. Compassion opens our hearts and enables us to transcend envy, allowing us to rejoice in others' successes rather than feel jealousy. Through compassion, we align with our higher nature and cultivate peaceful, harmonious relationships.

Relevance

By cultivating compassion, we replace envy with joy and gratitude, recognizing others as reflections of the divine. This leads to spiritual fulfillment, inner peace, and harmony in our interactions.

End of Day 12

Summary:

- Today, you identified moments of envy and consciously replaced them with compassion.
- You learned that by focusing on the well-being and success of others, you can let go of resentment and foster a more positive mindset.

14

Day 13: Seeking Truth and Clarity to Overcome Delusion

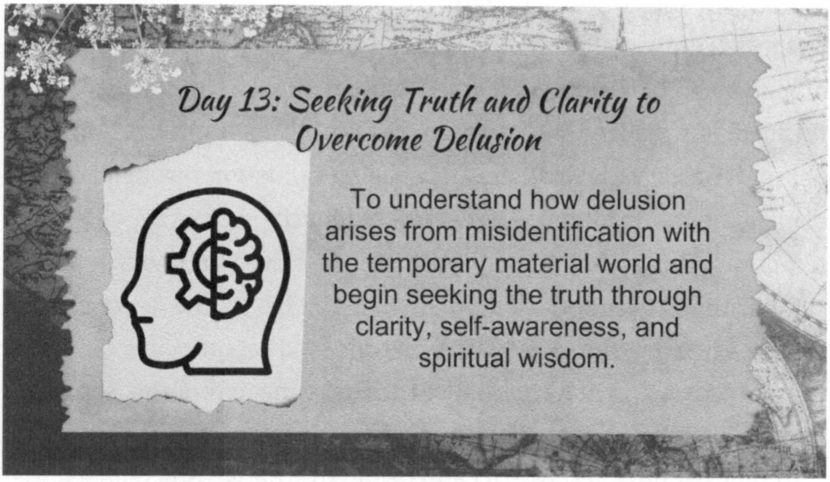

Purpose: To understand how delusion arises from misidentification with the temporary material world and begin seeking the truth through clarity, self-awareness, and spiritual wisdom.

Anjali's Window of Clarity

Anjali had always been ambitious. She worked in a high-profile corporate role, and over the years, she had accumulated a comfortable lifestyle—designer clothes, a luxury car, and frequent vacations. On the outside, everything looked perfect. Yet, lately, she had begun to feel an unsettling emptiness. Despite achieving every milestone she had set for herself, she noticed a lingering sense of dissatisfaction.

One evening, as she scrolled through social media, Anjali felt a pang of inadequacy. Her friends seemed happier, more accomplished, more fulfilled. She realized she had been measuring her worth by comparing her material success to others and chasing validation through external achievements. It hit her—her sense of identity was wrapped around temporary things, and it wasn't bringing her true happiness.

Determined to find clarity, Anjali took a step back the next morning. She set aside her phone, left work on time, and sat quietly in her living room, focusing on her breath. For the first time in months, she asked herself: *Who am I beyond my job, my possessions, my status?*

In that stillness, a sense of calm began to emerge. She realized that her identity was not in her promotions, her salary, or the applause of others. Her true self was the inner awareness that had always been present—the part of her that experienced love, peace, and connection regardless of circumstances.

Later, at work, a client meeting didn't go as planned, and normally Anjali would have felt frustrated and stressed. But this time, she paused, took a deep breath, and reminded herself: *This outcome does not define me. My true self is beyond success or failure.* In that moment, she felt a profound clarity and lightness she hadn't experienced in a long time.

That evening, she journaled her reflections. She wrote about the delusions she had been living under—mistaking temporary success for true identity—and the liberation she felt from seeing her inner truth. Anjali realized that seeking truth and clarity was not a one-time event but a daily practice. By connecting with her inner self, she could rise above the illusions of material life and find lasting peace.

By the end of the day, Anjali felt a quiet joy and a sense of freedom. She understood that the world of material achievements and comparisons would always exist, but her true fulfillment came from aligning with her inner truth and living with clarity.

Like Anjali, we often fall into the delusion of identifying ourselves with temporary things. Today, notice where you might be caught in such illusions. Take a moment to pause, breathe, and reflect on your true self beyond material possessions, status, or approval from others. By seeking truth and clarity, you can overcome delusion and cultivate lasting peace and inner fulfillment.

1. Understand the Concept of Delusion (Misidentification with the Material and Temporary)

- **Action:** Delusion occurs when we misidentify ourselves with material possessions, status, or transient experiences. We often believe that external circumstances or temporary things define our true identity and purpose.
- **Simple Explanation:** Delusion = The mistaken belief that the material world, fleeting pleasures, and external achievements are the source of lasting fulfillment or our true self.

Example: I used to think that accumulating wealth and success would bring me lasting happiness, but I often felt empty even after achieving those goals. I realized this was a form of delusion because true happiness comes from within, not from external factors.

2. Recognize Areas of Delusion in Your Life

- **Action:** Reflect on areas in your life where you may be holding onto misperceptions about your identity, happiness, or purpose.

Ask yourself:

- Where do I place my sense of worth or identity?
- Am I clinging to material things or external validations for my happiness?
- **Write down** three specific areas in your life where you have been misidentifying your true self with material or temporary things.

Examples:

1. *I used to define my success by how much money I made, thinking that financial stability would bring me peace of mind. I now realize that true peace comes from within, not from external wealth.*
2. *I often equated my happiness with how many likes and comments I got on social media, believing that online approval defined my value.*
3. *I believed that my worth was tied to the approval of others, especially my family, and that their validation would give me a sense of purpose.*

3. Seek Truth and Clarity

- **Action:** Begin seeking clarity about your true nature beyond the material world. Reflect on your inner essence, purpose, and connection to the divine or higher self.

Today, practice these actions:

- Spend time in quiet contemplation or meditation, focusing on the truth of who you really are.
- Read spiritual texts, listen to teachings, or engage in activities that expand your understanding of your true nature.
- Observe moments when you get caught up in material pursuits and gently remind yourself that these are temporary, and true fulfillment lies in deeper awareness.

Example: During meditation, I focused on the awareness that I am not my possessions or achievements. I am a soul, connected to the divine, and this realization brought me peace. I also noticed that I no longer felt as attached to the outcome of my career goals, understanding that my true purpose lies in spiritual growth, not material success.

4. Set an Intention to Live by the Truth

- **Action:** Today, choose one situation where you typically get caught up in material or temporary concerns, and consciously practice seeing it through the lens of truth.
- For example: If you feel stress or frustration about your career or material possessions, pause and remind yourself that these things are transient and do not define your true self. Seek clarity about your deeper purpose in that moment.
- Take a deep breath and affirm: *"I am more than my external circumstances. My true self is eternal and connected to a higher purpose."*

Example: Today, when I felt overwhelmed about not meeting a career goal, I paused and reminded myself that this goal is not my true identity. I focused on reconnecting with my inner peace and remembering that true fulfillment comes from within.

5. Evening Reflection (Journaling)

- **Action:** Before ending your day, write down your reflections on how you sought truth and clarity today. Use these questions as a guide:
- How did it feel to reflect on your true self beyond material pursuits?
- *Example: It felt liberating to remind myself that I am not my job or possessions. It allowed me to detach from stress and focus on my spiritual growth.*
- In what areas of your life did you notice delusion arising today?
- *Example: I noticed that I was getting frustrated because my car broke down. I realized I was placing too much importance on this material possession.*
- How did you seek truth or clarity in those moments?
- *Example: I took a few minutes to meditate and remind myself that I am not my car. I found clarity in knowing that my true worth comes from my inner peace, not material things.*
- Did you feel any shift in your perspective after seeking truth?
- *Example: Yes, I felt a shift in perspective. I stopped worrying about the material issue and focused on my spiritual growth and well-being.*
- What is your takeaway about how delusion has affected your life, and how truth brings clarity?
- *Example: I realized that I often seek fulfillment in external things, but true peace and clarity come from understanding that I am a soul, not the material things I have. This awareness helped me feel more at ease with life's challenges.*

Guided by Bhagavad Gita Wisdom

Krishna emphasizes the importance of seeking truth and living in alignment with it. In the Bhagavad Gita (4.34), He says:

"Learn the truth by approaching a spiritual master. Inquire submissively and render service unto such a person. The self-realized souls can impart knowledge unto you because they have seen the truth."

This verse highlights that by approaching a realized teacher with humility and devotion, we can gain true knowledge, which dispels the delusions of the material world. Understanding this truth reveals our eternal nature, helping us rise above worldly attachments and misconceptions.

Relevance

Seeking truth dissolves the illusions of the material world, allowing us to recognize our eternal soul and divine purpose. This leads to clarity, spiritual wisdom, and lasting inner peace.

End of Day 13

Summary:

- Today, you recognized areas where delusion affects your life, and you sought truth and clarity by reflecting on your true self beyond the material world.
- By embracing your deeper spiritual nature, you took a significant step toward overcoming delusion and gaining greater clarity in life.

15

Day 14: Weekly Reflection: Tracking Shifts in Thoughts and Behavior

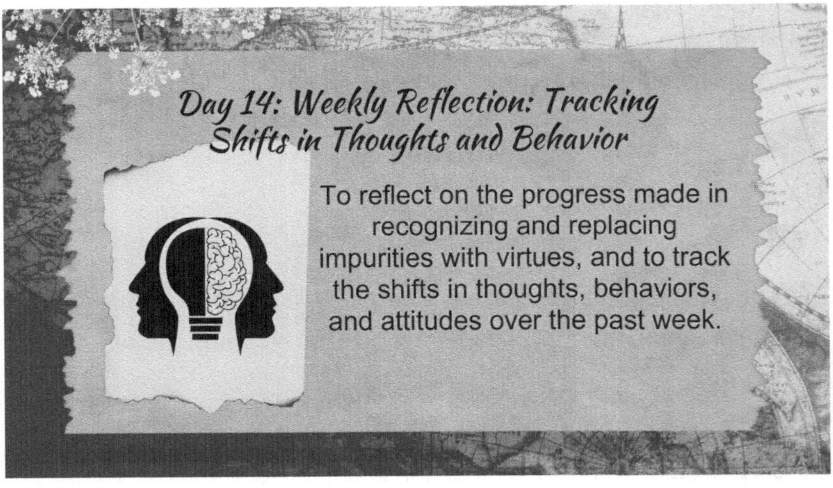

Purpose: To reflect on the progress made in recognizing and replacing impurities with virtues, and to track the shifts in thoughts, behaviors, and attitudes over the past week.

Avantika's Week of Transformation

Avantika had spent the past two weeks on a journey of self-awareness. At first, she had barely noticed how often her mind was caught up in lustful desires, anger, greed, pride, envy, and delusion. But after committing to the daily practices, she began to see subtle yet meaningful changes in her thoughts, emotions, and actions.

On this Sunday evening, she decided to sit quietly with her journal, reflecting on her week. She thought about Monday, when she had felt a surge of anger at a colleague's careless mistake. Normally, she would have snapped or criticized sharply. But this week, she had paused, taken a deep breath, and responded with patience. She remembered how good it felt to see the situation resolve without conflict.

She smiled as she recalled Tuesday, when envy had surfaced at the praise a friend received for a presentation. Instead of comparing herself, she had congratulated them sincerely, and in that moment, she realized her own excitement for their success brought unexpected joy. By Wednesday, she noticed moments of pride creeping in when her manager complimented her work. She had chosen humility, appreciating the contributions of her teammates alongside her own, and felt a sense of balance.

Avantika wrote down her reflections for each day, acknowledging where she had succeeded and where she had struggled. She noticed that practicing contentment reduced her anxious desire for more, and cultivating compassion improved her relationships. Some moments were still challenging—she caught herself slipping into old patterns of greed or frustration—but she no longer felt defeated. Each pause, each conscious choice, was a small victory that accumulated into meaningful progress.

By the end of her reflection, Avantika felt a quiet pride—not the ego-driven kind, but a deep, steady sense of accomplishment. She realized that tracking her thoughts and behaviors had transformed awareness into wisdom. The week had shown her that change doesn't happen overnight; it unfolds through persistent attention, self-discipline, and conscious choices.

With a calm smile, she closed her journal and set a simple intention for the coming week: to continue observing, reflecting, and aligning her actions with the virtues she had been cultivating. She felt motivated, peaceful, and connected to her journey, knowing that each small step was a seed for lasting transformation.

Like Avantika, take this day to pause and observe the shifts in your thoughts and behaviors. Celebrate the progress you've made, acknowledge the areas where you still need growth, and set an intention to continue your journey of self-awareness and virtue. Each reflection deepens your understanding, strengthens your habits, and brings clarity to your path of inner transformation.

1. Reflect on Your Awareness of Impurities

- **Action:** Take a moment to review the past week and reflect on how aware you have become of your negative tendencies and impurities, such as lust, anger, greed, pride, envy, and delusion.

Ask yourself:

- Which impurities did I become more aware of this week?

- How did I notice them arising in my thoughts and behaviors?

Example: I became more aware of my anger arising in certain situations, especially when my expectations weren't met. I noticed that I would react impulsively, but I was able to pause and choose a calmer response.

2. Track Shifts in Your Thoughts and Behavior

- **Action:** Reflect on the shifts you experienced in your thoughts and behaviors over the week, especially in situations where you worked on replacing negative tendencies with their opposite virtues.

Ask yourself:

- What positive shifts did I notice in my thoughts and behaviors?
- How did I begin responding differently to situations that previously triggered negative emotions?
- **Write down** any specific changes you've noticed.

Examples:

- *I noticed that when I felt the urge to compare myself to others, I consciously chose to practice compassion instead of envy. I felt more connected and at peace with myself.*
- *Instead of reacting with frustration when I didn't get what I wanted, I practiced humility and accepted the situation with grace.*
- *When I felt greedy or focused on material gain, I reminded myself to focus on contentment, which helped me feel more fulfilled and at ease.*

3. Reflect on the Impact of These Shifts

- **Action:** Consider the impact these shifts in thoughts and behavior have had on your emotional well-being and relationships.

Ask yourself:

- How have these changes affected my inner peace and contentment?
- What effect have these changes had on my relationships with others?
- **Write down** your reflections.

Examples:

- *By practicing contentment, I've noticed that I feel less stressed about external circumstances and more at peace with what I have. I am less anxious and more grateful.*
- *When I practiced humility, I felt a deeper connection with my colleagues. There was less competition and more collaboration in the workplace.*
- *Forgiving myself and others has given me a sense of emotional freedom. I no longer hold onto anger or resentment, and I feel lighter and more compassionate.*

4. Identify Areas for Continued Growth

- **Action:** Reflect on any areas where you still feel a tendency to fall into negative thoughts or behaviors.

Ask yourself:

- Where did I struggle this week?
- In what situations did I find it difficult to apply the virtues I'm trying

to cultivate?

- **Write down** these areas of struggle and set an intention to continue working on them in the coming week.

Examples:

- *I noticed that when I was dealing with a stressful situation at work, I became frustrated and impatient. I struggled to maintain contentment and felt overwhelmed.*
- *I found it hard to practice forgiveness in moments when I felt betrayed by others. I need to focus more on compassion in those moments.*
- *I sometimes still have moments where I feel inferior to others, especially when I compare myself to my peers. I need to continue practicing humility in these situations.*

5. Celebrate Your Progress

- **Action:** Take a moment to acknowledge and celebrate your growth over the past week, no matter how small.

Ask yourself:

- What am I proud of accomplishing this week?
- What positive changes have I noticed in my attitude or behavior?
- **Write down** the progress you've made and celebrate your commitment to this journey.

Examples:

- *I'm proud of myself for recognizing and managing my anger in difficult situations. I've become more patient and calm.*

- *I feel a sense of accomplishment in replacing envy with compassion. I now focus more on building positive connections instead of comparing myself to others.*
- *I'm grateful for the shifts I've made towards contentment. I'm not as driven by external success, and I'm learning to enjoy the present moment.*

6. Evening Reflection (Journaling)

- **Action:** Before ending your day, write down your reflections on the week. Use these questions to guide you:
- What is the most significant shift I've noticed in myself this week?
- *Example: The most significant shift has been learning to pause and respond with calmness instead of reacting impulsively when things don't go as planned.*
- How have my relationships been impacted by these changes?
- *Example: My relationships feel more harmonious because I've practiced forgiveness and humility. I'm less focused on my ego and more on understanding others.*
- What area will I focus on improving in the next week?
- *Example: Next week, I want to focus on practicing contentment even more, especially in situations where I feel the urge to strive for more or compare myself to others.*
- How do I feel about my progress on this journey?
- *Example: I feel encouraged and grateful. I've made meaningful progress, and I'm excited to continue on this path of self-improvement.*

Guided by Bhagavad Gita Wisdom

Krishna emphasizes the importance of self-reflection and disciplined effort in the Bhagavad Gita (6.5). He says:

"One must elevate oneself by one's own mind, not degrade oneself, for the mind alone is the friend of the self, and the mind alone is the enemy of the self."

This verse highlights that spiritual progress depends on conscious self-awareness and introspection. By observing our thoughts, behaviors, and tendencies, we can guide the mind toward positive action, refine our habits, and overcome negative impulses. Self-reflection allows us to recognize subtle shifts in consciousness and align with our higher nature.

Relevance

This day offers a moment to pause and observe the changes that have occurred so far. Tracking our thoughts and behaviors through reflection deepens self-awareness, strengthens virtues, and provides clarity for further growth on the spiritual path.

End of Day 14

Summary:

- Today, you reflected on the shifts in your thoughts and behaviors over the past week, tracking your progress in recognizing and replacing negative tendencies with positive virtues.
- By identifying areas of growth and areas for continued improvement, you are setting the stage for continued transformation and purification of the mind and heart.

16

Day 15: Detaching from Desires Through Self-Discipline

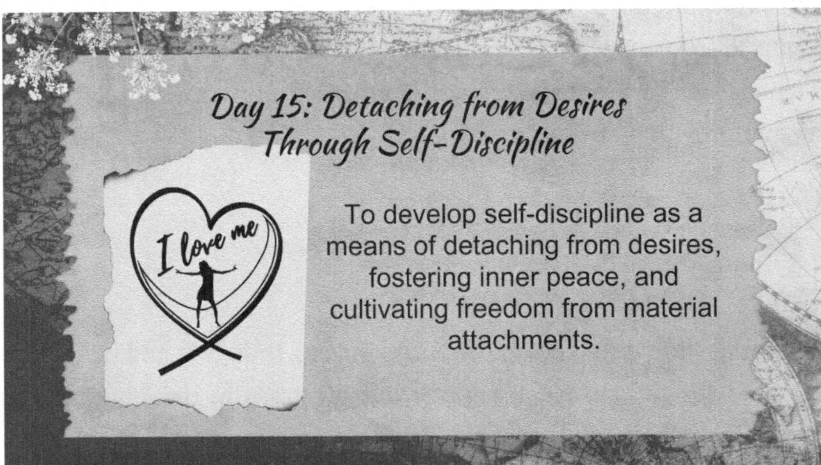

Purpose: To develop self-discipline as a means of detaching from desires, fostering inner peace, and cultivating freedom from material attachments.

Aarav and the Golden Hour

Aarav loved the quiet of early mornings. For years, he had tried to use that "golden hour" before work to meditate, read, or reflect—but somehow, every morning, he found himself scrolling endlessly through his phone, checking messages, news, and social media updates. The time he had set aside for inner peace quietly slipped away.

One morning, Aarav decided to try something different. Before going to bed, he placed his phone in another room, out of reach. As soon as his alarm rang, a familiar urge stirred within him. He felt restless and bored without his usual morning scroll. His mind raced with thoughts: "What if I miss an important message? What if something happens?"

He realized this was more than just a habit—it was a desire for constant stimulation, a subtle craving to feel connected, informed, and validated. Aarav took a deep breath and reminded himself: "This is my moment to choose freedom, not indulgence."

With determination, he sat on his meditation cushion and focused on his breath. At first, the restlessness persisted, but gradually, he noticed a sense of calm washing over him. Without the pull of his usual distractions, he could hear his own thoughts clearly, observe them without reacting, and feel a lightness he hadn't experienced in a long time.

Later, Aarav reflected on the experience. He realized that self-discipline wasn't about punishing himself or eliminating pleasures—it was about taking conscious control over desires that pull him away from inner peace. By practicing small acts of discipline, like leaving the phone aside, he could create space for clarity, focus, and freedom from attachments.

He thought about other areas in his life where desires had quietly taken control—impulse shopping, overconsumption of snacks, or seeking approval at work—and felt motivated to create small, practical plans to exercise self-discipline there too. Aarav smiled, feeling empowered. The golden hour was no longer just a time of day—it had become a symbol of his ability to detach, choose mindfully, and nurture inner peace.

Like Aarav, many of us allow desires to quietly guide our actions, stealing our attention and energy. Today, we begin by noticing these subtle cravings, creating small disciplines to manage them, and discovering the freedom that comes from conscious detachment.

1. Understand the Role of Self-Discipline in Detachment

- **Action:** Reflect on the importance of self-discipline in detaching from desires and creating a life of inner peace and balance.
- **Simple Explanation:** Self-discipline helps us manage our desires by training the mind and senses to avoid overindulgence and attachment to temporary pleasures.
- **Ask Yourself:**
- How does self-discipline help me detach from my desires?
- What areas of my life require more discipline to help me let go of unhelpful desires?

Example: Self-discipline helps me create healthy boundaries for my desires, like limiting time on social media to avoid unnecessary comparisons and distractions.

2. Identify Desires That Lead to Attachment

- **Action:** Reflect on the desires that often lead to attachment and create imbalance in your life.
- **Ask Yourself:**
- Which desires pull me away from my higher purpose or inner peace?
- Where do I tend to overindulge or allow my desires to control me?
- **Write down** three desires that you feel are leading you away from balance and inner peace.

Examples:

- *I have a desire for constant validation through social media likes and comments.*
- *I desire material possessions and often find myself buying things I don't truly need.*
- *I crave approval from others, especially in my work, and that desire makes me feel insecure.*

3. Develop a Plan for Self-Discipline

- **Action:** Create a specific plan for practicing self-discipline to detach from these desires and cultivate inner peace.
- **Ask Yourself:**
- What steps can I take to reduce attachment to these desires?
- What small, disciplined actions can I take today to detach from these desires?
- **Write down** one or two specific actions you can take to exercise self-discipline.

Examples:

- *I will reduce my social media usage to 30 minutes per day, setting a timer to help me stay accountable.*
- *I will avoid impulsive purchases by creating a shopping list and sticking to it when I go to the store.*
- *I will practice self-affirmation daily, reminding myself that my worth does not depend on the approval of others.*

4. Practice Self-Discipline in Action

- **Action:** For the next 24 hours, practice one of the self-discipline actions you've identified, and observe how it feels.
- **Ask Yourself:**
- How does it feel to practice self-discipline in this area?
- What challenges do I face when trying to detach from this desire?
- **Write down** your experiences with practicing self-discipline, focusing on both the challenges and the successes.

Examples:

- *Today, I practiced limiting my social media time to 30 minutes. It felt difficult at first, but I noticed that I had more time for other activities and felt less distracted.*
- *I stuck to my shopping list and didn't buy anything unnecessary. I felt empowered and content with my choices.*
- *I took time to affirm my self-worth without relying on external validation. It made me feel more secure in who I am.*

5. Reflect on the Results of Your Practice

- **Action:** At the end of the day, reflect on the results of your self-discipline practice and how it affected your mindset and well-being.
- **Ask Yourself:**
- What impact did practicing self-discipline have on my desires and attachments?
- How did I feel when I was able to detach from these desires?
- **Write down** your reflections on the positive effects of practicing self-discipline and detaching from desires.

Examples:

- *By limiting my social media usage, I felt more present in my real-life interactions and less concerned with others' opinions.*
- *Avoiding unnecessary purchases helped me feel more in control of my finances and less attached to material things.*
- *Practicing self-affirmation helped me feel more grounded in my identity, reducing my need for external validation.*

6. Evening Reflection (Journaling)

- **Action:** Before ending your day, write down your reflections on how practicing self-discipline to detach from desires affected you today. Use these questions to guide you:
- What was my experience with detaching from desires through self-discipline?
- *Example: Today, I found it challenging but liberating to detach from my desire for constant validation. I felt more at peace and less driven by external approval.*

- How did I feel when I exercised self-discipline?
- *Example: I felt proud of myself for sticking to my self-imposed limits, and I noticed a sense of calm and satisfaction.*
- What areas can I continue to work on for further detachment?
- *Example: I still need to work on reducing my attachment to material possessions. I will continue practicing mindful spending.*
- What did I learn about my desires and how they affect me?
- *Example: I realized that many of my desires are driven by external influences, not true needs. By practicing self-discipline, I can regain control over them.*

Guided by Bhagavad Gita Wisdom

Krishna emphasizes the importance of self-discipline (*yoga*) in controlling desires in the Bhagavad Gita (6.5):

"One must elevate oneself by one's own mind, not degrade oneself; for the mind alone is the friend of the self, and the mind alone is the enemy of the self."

This verse highlights that mastery over the mind through disciplined practice is essential to overcome the pull of fleeting desires. By cultivating self-discipline, we learn to detach from temporary cravings and develop inner stability, clarity, and peace. The mind, when trained, becomes a supportive ally rather than a source of distraction or suffering.

Relevance

Practicing self-discipline helps us regulate our desires, focus on what truly matters, and create space for spiritual growth. Detaching from momentary impulses allows the mind to remain steady, bringing freedom, inner peace, and alignment with our higher purpose.

End of Day 15

Summary:

- Today, you practiced self-discipline to detach from desires that lead to attachment and imbalance. You developed an actionable plan to reduce these attachments and observed the positive effects of these practices.
- By continuing to cultivate self-discipline, you are strengthening your ability to remain detached from fleeting desires and focusing on your inner peace and spiritual growth.

17

Day 16: Observing Detachment from Outcomes (Nishkam Karma)

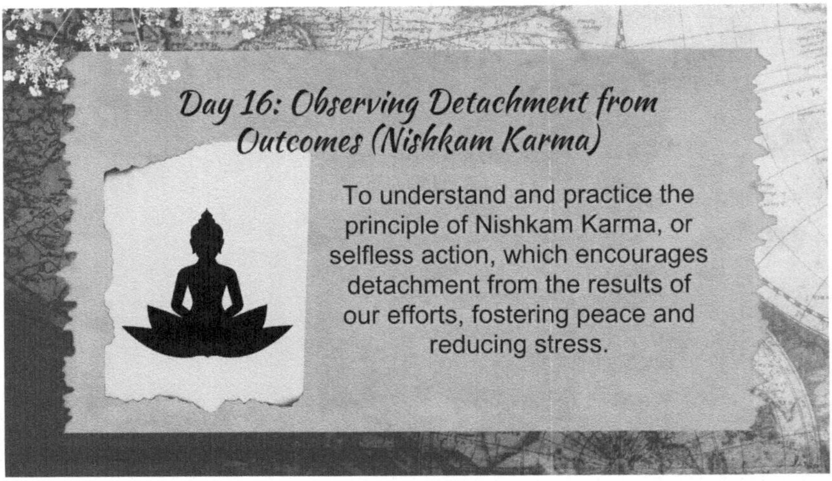

Purpose: To understand and practice the principle of Nishkam Karma, or selfless action, which encourages detachment from the results of our efforts, fostering peace and reducing stress.

Kavya and the Unfinished Painting

Kavya loved painting. For weeks, she had been working on a landscape that she imagined would be perfect—a painting that she hoped would impress her friends, family, and even the local art club. She planned every detail meticulously: the colors, the lighting, the smallest textures.

But as she painted, she began to feel tense. Every brushstroke brought a tiny worry: "Will this look good enough?" "What if it's not appreciated?" "Am I wasting my time if no one likes it?" The joy she once felt in painting was slowly being replaced by stress and self-doubt.

One afternoon, feeling frustrated, Kavya closed her eyes and took a deep breath. She remembered a teaching she had read from the Bhagavad Gita: the principle of Nishkam Karma—acting without attachment to results. "It's not the outcome, but the effort and intention that matter," she whispered to herself.

She decided to try something different. Instead of focusing on how the painting would be received, she focused on the act of painting itself—the feel of the brush on the canvas, the blending of colors, the quiet rhythm of her movements. Slowly, tension melted from her shoulders. Her mind, once crowded with expectations, became calm and attentive to the process.

By the end of the afternoon, the painting was far from perfect. Some colors blended unevenly, and certain lines didn't match her original vision. Yet, Kavya felt lighter, freer, and more joyful than she had in weeks. She realized that the stress and frustration had come not from the act of painting itself, but from her attachment to the outcome.

Kavya smiled, understanding something profound: when she acted selflessly—focused on her effort rather than the reward—she could find peace, joy, and fulfillment in every action. She decided to carry this awareness into all areas of her life: at work, in relationships, and in her creative pursuits. The results, she knew now, were not hers to control—but her effort, attention, and intention were.

Like Kavya, many of us tie our peace and happiness to the results of our efforts, only to feel stress, disappointment, or frustration. Today, we begin by observing where we cling to outcomes, practicing selfless action, and finding freedom in focusing on the process rather than the reward.

1. Understand the Concept of Nishkam Karma (Selfless Action)

- **Action:** Reflect on the Bhagavad Gita's teaching of Nishkam Karma, which is acting without attachment to the outcomes of our actions.
- **Simple Explanation:** Nishkam Karma means performing actions without getting attached to the results. This helps us to act with integrity, focusing on the process, not the outcome.
- **Example:***When I focus on the effort and not the outcome, I feel lighter, and I can put in my best without the stress of worrying about success or failure.*

2. Identify Situations Where You Are Attached to Outcomes

- **Action:** Reflect on situations in your life where you tend to become overly attached to the results, creating stress or disappointment when things don't go as planned.
- **Ask Yourself:**

- When do I get overly concerned with the outcome of my actions?
- What specific results am I attached to, and how does it affect my emotions and actions?
- **Write down** 3 recent situations where you were attached to a specific outcome.

Examples:

- *I was focused on getting a promotion at work and felt frustrated when I didn't get it.*
- *I felt anxious about how my book would be received and worried about others' opinions.*
- *I became upset when a project I was leading did not go as planned, feeling like I failed.*

3. Reflect on How Attachment to Outcomes Affects Your Peace

- **Action:** Reflect on how your attachment to results impacts your inner peace, mental well-being, and emotional state.
- **Ask Yourself:**
- How do I feel when my desired outcome doesn't materialize?
- How does being attached to outcomes affect my mood, energy, or peace of mind?
- **Write down** your reflections on how attachment to outcomes impacts your emotions and overall sense of peace.

Examples:

- *When I didn't get the promotion, I felt deflated, stressed, and uncertain about my worth.*

- *Worrying about how others would judge my book made me anxious and took away my joy in writing.*
- *When the project didn't succeed, I felt frustrated and defeated, even though I gave my best effort.*

4. Practice Acting Without Attachment to Results

- **Action:** Choose one situation today where you can practice detaching from the outcome and focusing solely on doing your best.
- **Ask Yourself:**
- How can I give my best effort in this situation without getting attached to the result?
- What actions can I take to release my expectations and remain focused on the process rather than the outcome?
- **Write down** how you will practice detachment from the outcome today.

Examples:

- *I will focus on doing my best at work without obsessing over whether I get a promotion.*
- *I will focus on writing my book for the joy of the process, not worrying about how it will be received.*
- *I will give my best to my project, but I will let go of the expectation of perfection or a particular result.*

5. Observe Your Reactions to Detachment from Outcomes

- **Action:** For the next 12 hours, observe your reactions as you practice detaching from outcomes. Pay attention to any moments when you feel the urge to get attached to results.

- **Ask Yourself:**
- How does it feel to focus on the process rather than the result?
- What thoughts or emotions arise when I try to detach from outcomes?
- **Write down** any moments of attachment or detachment you notice throughout the day.

Examples:

- *When I was working on a task, I noticed I was no longer stressed about whether I'd get a promotion. It felt liberating to just do my best.*
- *While writing, I felt free from the pressure of trying to make the book a success. It was easier to be creative and enjoy the process.*
- *I observed my mind wanting to control the results of a project, but I reminded myself that the outcome isn't in my hands and focused on doing my best instead.*

6. Evening Reflection (Journaling)

- **Action:** Before ending your day, reflect on your practice of detachment from outcomes. Here are some guiding questions to help structure your journaling:
- What was my experience of detaching from the outcome today?
- *Example: I felt freer and less stressed when I focused on doing my best without worrying about the outcome. I was more present and less anxious.*
- How did it feel when I let go of the need to control results?
- *Example: Letting go of the need to control the outcome gave me a sense*

of peace and calm. I felt more at ease and less burdened.

- What did I learn about my attachment to results?
- *Example: I realized that my attachment to outcomes often stems from insecurity. When I detach, I feel more confident and in control of my emotions.*
- How can I continue to practice Nishkam Karma moving forward?
- *Example: I can continue to focus on the process and trust that the results will follow. I will keep practicing this detachment in every area of my life.*

Guided by Bhagavad Gita Wisdom

Krishna teaches the principle of Nishkam Karma in the Bhagavad Gita (3.19):

"Therefore, without being attached to the fruits of activities, one should act as a matter of duty, for by working without attachment, one attains the Supreme."

This verse emphasizes performing our duties with dedication while letting go of expectations about the results. When we focus on the action itself, rather than its outcome, we free ourselves from stress, disappointment, and anxiety. Detachment from results cultivates inner calm, steadiness, and clarity of mind.

Relevance

By practicing Nishkam Karma, we learn to act selflessly and mindfully. This allows us to enjoy the process, put forth our best effort, and trust that outcomes are beyond our control. Over time, this approach strengthens inner peace, reduces frustration, and aligns our actions with our higher purpose.

End of Day 16

Summary:

- Today, you practiced detachment from the outcomes of your actions by embracing the concept of Nishkam Karma. You observed how attachment to results affects your peace and took steps to focus on the process rather than the result.
- By continuing to act without attachment to the fruits of your labor, you will cultivate a sense of peace, freedom, and contentment, regardless of external circumstances.

18

Day 17: Practicing Gratitude to Strengthen Purity of Mind

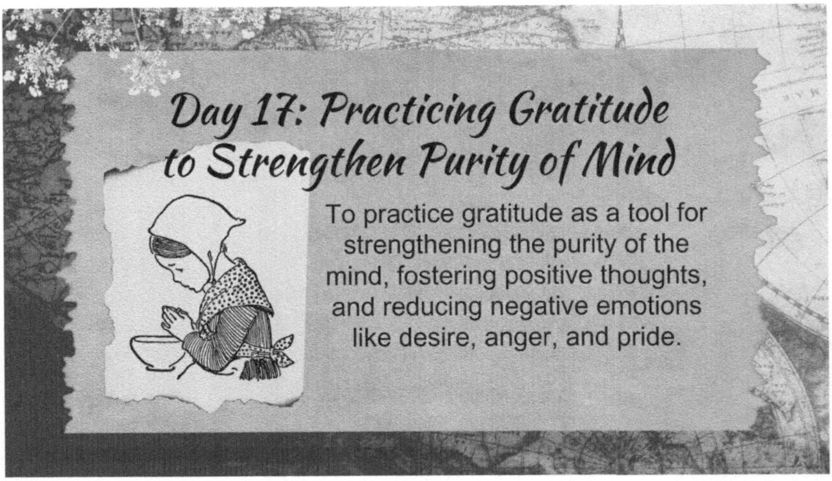

Purpose: To practice gratitude as a tool for strengthening the purity of the mind, fostering positive thoughts, and reducing negative emotions like desire, anger, and pride.

Neha's Gratitude Journal

Neha had always been a perfectionist. She worked long hours at her job, constantly comparing herself to colleagues, and frequently feeling frustrated when things didn't go as planned. Even small setbacks—like a delayed email or a missed deadline—would pull her into a spiral of stress and irritation.

One morning, feeling overwhelmed, she remembered a simple exercise she had read about in the Bhagavad Gita: gratitude. "If I can focus on what I have rather than what I lack," she thought, "maybe I can find some peace in the chaos."

Neha decided to try it intentionally. She opened her notebook and wrote down three things she was grateful for that morning: her supportive parents, her health, and the small garden outside her window that bloomed in sunlight. As she wrote, she felt a subtle shift—a lightness, a warmth, a quiet smile forming on her lips.

Later that day, a frustrating situation arose at work. A colleague criticized a report she had spent hours preparing. Normally, Neha would have felt anger and disappointment, but she paused and consciously reflected: "I am grateful for the chance to improve my work and learn from this feedback." She noticed how quickly the irritation melted, replaced by calm focus and clarity.

Throughout the day, Neha kept practicing gratitude: appreciating a colleague's thoughtful gesture, enjoying a quiet cup of tea, noticing the birds singing outside her window. Each moment of thankfulness seemed to strengthen her mind, making her less reactive, less judgmental, and more at ease.

By evening, Neha realized something powerful: gratitude was not just a list of things to acknowledge—it was a lens that purified her thoughts, softened her emotions, and allowed her to experience life more fully. Instead of focusing on what she didn't have or what went wrong, she felt connected, abundant, and peaceful.

Neha smiled as she closed her gratitude journal. She understood that by practicing thankfulness every day—even in small ways—she could strengthen the purity of her mind, reduce negative emotions like frustration and pride, and cultivate a lasting sense of peace and contentment.

Like Neha, many of us get caught in the pull of challenges, setbacks, and desires. Today, we begin by noticing the blessings in our lives, consciously practicing gratitude, and allowing it to transform our mindset, emotions, and relationships.

1. Understand the Concept of Gratitude

- **Action:** Reflect on the power of gratitude and how it can positively influence your mindset, emotions, and relationships.
- **Simple Explanation:** Gratitude is the practice of appreciating what we have, recognizing the blessings in our lives, and expressing thankfulness. By focusing on what is good, we cultivate a pure and peaceful mind.
- **Example:***When I focus on the things I am grateful for, I feel more at peace, less stressed, and more connected to others.*

2. Identify Moments When You Can Practice Gratitude

- **Action:** Reflect on moments throughout your day where you can consciously practice gratitude, especially during challenges or moments of negativity.
- **Ask Yourself:**
- What are three things I can be grateful for in my life right now?
- How can I shift my perspective to find gratitude, even in difficult situations?
- **Write down** 3 specific situations where you can consciously practice gratitude today.

Examples:

- *I will express gratitude for my health, even though it may not be perfect.*
- *I will be thankful for the support I receive from my family, even when things feel stressful.*
- *I will choose to appreciate the small moments of joy throughout my day, like the beauty of nature or a kind gesture.*

3. Reflect on How Gratitude Affects Your Thoughts and Emotions

- **Action:** Take a moment to reflect on how practicing gratitude can shift your mindset, reducing negative thoughts and fostering a more positive outlook.
- **Ask Yourself:**
- How do I feel when I focus on gratitude?
- What thoughts or emotions arise when I express thanks?
- **Write down** your reflections on how gratitude influences your mental and emotional state.

Examples:

- *When I focus on gratitude, I feel more peaceful and content. Negative thoughts are replaced with positive ones.*
- *Gratitude helps me shift my mindset from lack to abundance, reducing stress and anxiety.*
- *When I express gratitude, I feel more connected to others and less isolated or frustrated.*

4. Practice Gratitude in Challenging Situations

- **Action:** Today, when you face a difficult or frustrating situation, pause and consciously practice gratitude.
- **Ask Yourself:**
- What can I be grateful for in this situation, even though it's challenging?
- How can I change my perspective to find something positive to appreciate?
- **Write down** how you can apply gratitude to a specific challenge you are currently facing.

Examples:

- *When I feel frustrated at work, I will remind myself to be grateful for the opportunity to grow and learn.*
- *If I encounter a difficult person, I will choose to appreciate their perspective, even if I don't agree with it.*
- *When I feel stressed about my responsibilities, I will take a moment to be thankful for the ability to manage them.*

5. Observe the Impact of Gratitude on Your Mindset

- **Action:** For the next 12 hours, pay attention to how your thoughts and emotions shift when you practice gratitude throughout your day.
- **Ask Yourself:**
- How does practicing gratitude affect my interactions with others?
- What shifts do I notice in my emotions and mental state after consciously practicing gratitude?
- **Write down** your observations on the impact of gratitude on your mindset.

Examples:

- *After practicing gratitude, I noticed I was more patient with my colleagues and felt less irritated by small inconveniences.*
- *Focusing on gratitude helped me feel more grounded and positive, even when challenges arose.*
- *I felt a deeper sense of contentment when I focused on the things I have, rather than what I lack.*

6. Evening Reflection (Journaling)

- **Action:** Before ending your day, reflect on your experience with practicing gratitude. Here are some guiding questions to help structure your journaling:
- How did I feel when I practiced gratitude today?
- *Example: I felt a sense of calm and joy when I focused on gratitude. It helped me feel more connected to myself and others.*
- Were there moments when gratitude helped shift my mindset during a challenge?
- *Example: When I felt overwhelmed, practicing gratitude helped me find*

peace and focus on what truly matters.

- What did I learn about the role of gratitude in purifying the mind?
- *Example: I realized that gratitude helps clear my mind of negative thoughts, making space for peace and positivity.*
- How can I make gratitude a more regular part of my daily life?
- *Example: I will make a habit of reflecting on three things I'm grateful for every morning, to start my day with a positive mindset.*

Guided by Bhagavad Gita Wisdom

Gratitude is a key element in purifying the mind. Krishna emphasizes the importance of devotion and thankfulness for the divine in the Bhagavad Gita (9.22), saying:

"To those who are constantly devoted and who worship Me with love, I give the understanding by which they can come to Me."

This teaches that expressing gratitude opens the mind to divine guidance and support. Gratitude aligns the mind with divine grace, shifting our focus from scarcity to abundance.

Relevance

By practicing gratitude, we strengthen the purity of the mind and soul, opening ourselves to divine grace and cultivating positive energy, which aids in our spiritual growth.

End of Day 17

Summary:

- Today, you practiced gratitude as a means of strengthening the purity of your mind. By focusing on what is good in your life, you cultivated a positive mindset and reduced negative emotions.
- Gratitude is a powerful tool for fostering peace, joy, and content-

ment, and it helps create a clearer, more positive mental state.

19

Day 18: Balancing Energy: Removing Tamas (Inertia and Ignorance)

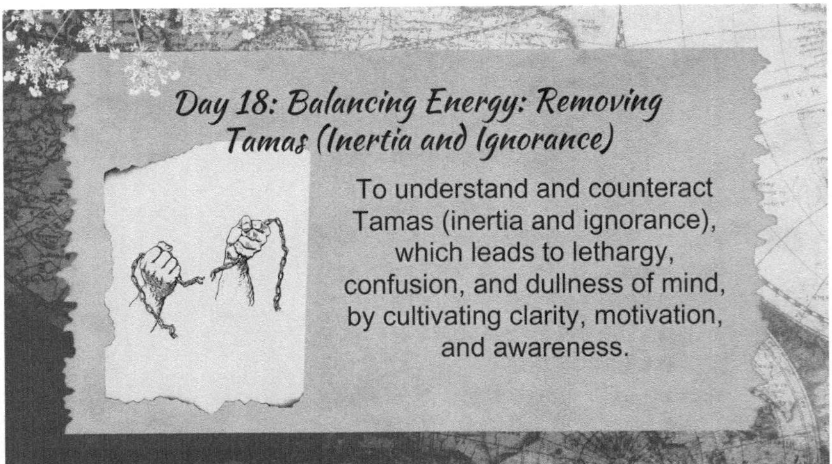

Purpose: To understand and counteract Tamas (inertia and ignorance), which leads to lethargy, confusion, and dullness of mind, by cultivating clarity, motivation, and awareness.

Sameer and the Morning Fog

Sameer had always prided himself on being disciplined, but lately, he felt stuck. Mornings were the hardest. Even after sleeping well, he woke up feeling heavy, unmotivated, and mentally foggy. Tasks he normally handled with ease now felt like mountains, and he found himself scrolling aimlessly on his phone instead of starting his day.

One morning, Sameer noticed something different. As he sat at his desk, staring blankly at his to-do list, he realized: this fog, this lack of energy—it wasn't just tiredness. It was Tamas, the inertia and dullness that Krishna describes in the Bhagavad Gita. He felt mentally sluggish, disconnected from purpose, and aware that this inertia was silently shaping his day.

Determined to break the cycle, Sameer decided to take action. He started with a brisk walk outside, feeling the cool air and sunlight touch his skin. Each step seemed to shake off the heaviness in his mind. Returning home, he organized his workspace, cleared piles of paper, and set one clear goal for the morning: to finish a small project he had been avoiding.

As he worked, he noticed a subtle but powerful shift. His mind felt sharper, his thoughts clearer, and his energy returning. He realized that Tamas had been clouding not only his productivity but also his mood and confidence. By intentionally engaging in movement, organizing his environment, and setting purposeful actions, he was cultivating awareness, clarity, and motivation.

Later, Sameer reflected on the day. He understood that inertia isn't something to blame—it's a signal. It reminds us when we need to bring awareness, energy, and intention into our actions. By noticing the fog, taking small positive steps, and staying mindful, he could gradually remove Tamas and restore balance in his life.

Sameer smiled as he prepared for the evening. The heaviness that had weighed him down in the morning had lifted, replaced by a sense of focus, vitality, and calm purpose. He realized that reducing Tamas wasn't a one-time effort—it was a daily practice of clarity, movement, and mindful action.

Like Sameer, many of us experience moments when inertia or confusion clouds our mind. Today, we begin by noticing Tamas, taking conscious steps to bring energy and clarity into our actions, and observing the transformative effect it has on our focus, motivation, and overall sense of well-being.

1. Understand the Concept of Tamas (Inertia and Ignorance)

- **Action:** Reflect on the qualities of Tamas—mental inertia, laziness, confusion, and ignorance. It is the state where we feel stuck, disengaged, or lack awareness.
- **Simple Explanation:** Tamas is the quality of darkness or heaviness that clouds the mind, making it harder to act, think clearly, or engage with life purposefully.
- **Example:***When I feel unmotivated and unable to focus, that's Tamas clouding my mind, keeping me from acting with clarity and purpose.*

2. Identify Moments of Tamas in Your Life

- **Action:** Reflect on moments from the past week when you felt mentally sluggish, uninspired, or unclear about your actions.

- **Ask Yourself:**
- When did I feel mentally foggy or lacking in energy?
- Was I avoiding tasks or feeling confused about what to do?
- **Write down** 3 specific situations in the past week where you noticed Tamas (inertia or ignorance) affecting your behavior or mindset.

Examples:

- *I felt physically tired and mentally foggy all day, unable to focus on my work.*
- *I found myself procrastinating and avoiding a difficult conversation I needed to have.*
- *I felt stuck and didn't know how to solve a problem at work, even though I had the resources to address it.*

3. Recognize the Effects of Tamas on Your Energy

- **Action:** Observe how Tamas affects your physical, mental, and emotional energy levels. Recognize the contrast between feeling clear, energized, and focused, versus feeling stuck and uninspired.
- **Ask Yourself:**
- How do I feel physically and mentally when I am in a state of inertia or confusion?
- How does Tamas impact my relationships and ability to function?
- **Write down** your observations about how Tamas influences your energy.

Examples:

- *When I feel lethargic, I notice my energy is low, and I lack the drive to complete important tasks.*
- *Tamas makes me feel disconnected from others and unsure of myself.*
- *My physical body feels heavy, and I often feel mentally foggy when I'm in a state of inertia.*

4. Cultivate Awareness and Motivation to Overcome Tamas

- **Action:** Today, set an intention to break free from the inertia of Tamas by engaging in activities that stimulate clarity, energy, and awareness.
- **Ask Yourself:**
- What activities can I engage in today to shake off mental fog and ignite energy in my mind and body?
- How can I bring awareness and intention into my actions, rather than letting inertia control me?
- **Write down** actions you will take today to overcome the inertia of Tamas.

Examples:

- *I will go for a walk or exercise to break the mental fog and stimulate my energy.*
- *I will take small, purposeful actions, like organizing my workspace or setting a clear goal for the day.*
- *I will pause for 5 minutes of meditation or deep breathing to center myself and bring clarity to my thoughts.*

5. Observe Shifts in Energy and Awareness

- **Action:** For the next 12 hours, pay attention to any changes in your energy levels, clarity, and awareness when you engage in activities that combat Tamas.
- **Ask Yourself:**
- How does my energy shift after engaging in positive, motivating activities?
- Do I notice increased mental clarity or reduced inertia?
- **Write down** your observations about how your energy and awareness shift after making an effort to overcome Tamas.

Examples:

- *After taking a brisk walk, I felt more energized and able to focus on tasks with greater clarity.*
- *By organizing my workspace, I felt a sense of accomplishment and was able to think more clearly.*
- *I noticed that after a few minutes of deep breathing, I was able to think more sharply and feel less overwhelmed by distractions.*

6. Evening Reflection (Journaling)

- **Action:** Before ending your day, reflect on your experience of overcoming Tamas. Here are some guiding questions to help structure your journaling:
- How did I feel when I noticed Tamas affecting my energy today?
- *Example: I felt sluggish in the morning and couldn't focus. It was frustrating to realize how much Tamas was affecting my productivity.*
- What steps did I take to overcome Tamas, and how did they help?
- *Example: I took a 10-minute walk and felt a shift in my energy, allowing me to get more done.*

- How did overcoming Tamas impact my clarity, energy, and mindset?
- *Example: When I made an effort to break free from inertia, I noticed that my mind became clearer and I felt more energized.*
- How can I continue to reduce Tamas in my life going forward?
- *Example: I will incorporate more movement into my day and set intentional goals to stay motivated and avoid mental fog.*

Guided by Bhagavad Gita Wisdom

Tamas represents inertia, ignorance, and dullness (*14.8*). In Chapter 14, Verse 8, Krishna describes the mode of darkness (Tamas) as being born of ignorance, leading to delusion in all embodied beings. This mode binds individuals through heedlessness, indolence, and sleep. Specifically, the verse states:

"But know thou Tamas to be born of ignorance, deluding all embodied beings; it binds fast, O Arjuna, through heedlessness, indolence, and sleep."

This verse highlights how Tamas manifests as mental inertia, confusion, and lethargy, which can cloud judgment and hinder spiritual progress.

Relevance

By recognizing and counteracting Tamas, we can cultivate clarity, motivation, and awareness. Engaging in purposeful actions, setting clear goals, and maintaining mindfulness can help overcome the inertia associated with Tamas. This proactive approach fosters a balanced and energized state of mind, essential for spiritual growth and well-being.

End of Day 18

Summary:

- Today, you identified moments when Tamas (inertia and ignorance) clouded your energy and clarity.
- You practiced engaging in actions that would help you overcome this inertia, such as physical activity, setting goals, and bringing awareness to your actions.
- Reducing Tamas is a key step in creating a clearer, more energized, and purposeful life.

20

Day 19: Balancing Energy: Moderating Rajas (Overactivity and Restlessness)

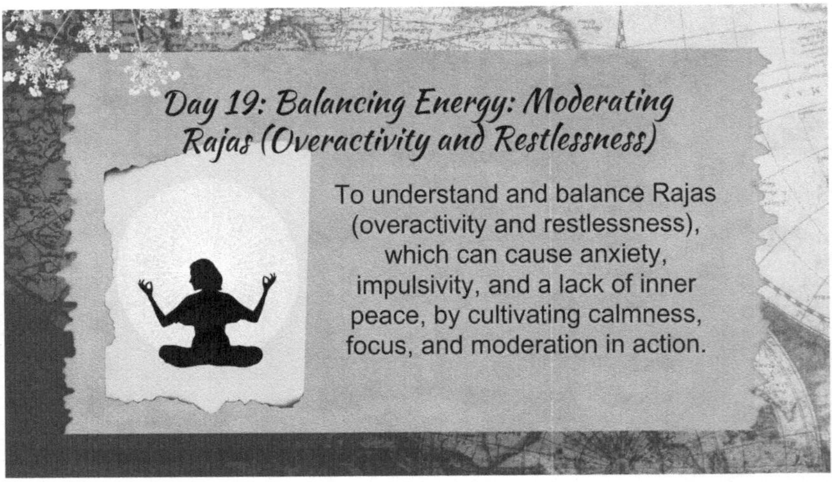

Purpose: To understand and balance Rajas (overactivity and restlessness), which can cause anxiety, impulsivity, and a lack of inner peace, by cultivating calmness, focus, and moderation in action.

Neel and the Restless Ventures

Neel was a driven entrepreneur, always looking for the next big business idea. Every month brought a new course to learn, a new business plan to explore, or a fresh investment opportunity. While his calendar was full and his resume impressive, Neel felt restless and unsatisfied. No matter how many ventures he started, a lingering anxiety followed him—he constantly feared missing out, never fully enjoying the present moment.

One morning, Neel found himself juggling three new projects, all half-finished, and dozens of courses he had signed up for but never completed. His energy felt scattered, his mind overactive, and even simple decisions became exhausting. He realized that his constant hopping from one venture to another—his inability to slow down—was draining him more than it was helping him grow. This was Rajas: the energy of overactivity, restlessness, and endless striving without contentment.

Determined to change, Neel decided to bring moderation and focus into his day. Instead of diving into a new idea, he chose one project to complete. He scheduled short breaks, practiced mindful breathing, and reminded himself to focus on the process rather than rushing to the next opportunity.

By midday, Neel noticed a shift. Tasks he had dreaded felt manageable. His mind was calmer, decisions became clearer, and his creativity flowed more freely. He realized that by moderating his actions and slowing down, he could achieve more with less stress—and finally enjoy the journey rather than just chasing the result.

In the evening, Neel reflected on his lesson: success is not measured by how many ventures you start, but by how fully and mindfully you engage in the work you do. Moderating Rajas didn't mean giving up ambition; it meant channeling energy wisely, balancing effort with calmness, and finding satisfaction in the present.

Like Neel, many of us fall into the trap of restlessness, believing that busyness equals success. Today, we begin by noticing when Rajas is at play, slowing down, focusing on one task at a time, and experiencing the clarity, peace, and energy that come from moderation.

1. Understand the Concept of Rajas (Overactivity and Restlessness)

- **Action:** Reflect on the qualities of Rajas—mental restlessness, excessive activity, anxiety, and the constant desire for more. It is the state of constant movement, agitation, and the desire to achieve, but without true satisfaction.
- **Simple Explanation:** Rajas is the quality of energy that drives activity, but when out of balance, it leads to stress, overexertion, and a sense of never being content with what we have.
- **Example:***When I feel restless and constantly rushing to get things done, without taking time to pause and reflect, that's Rajas in my life.*

2. Identify Moments of Rajas in Your Life

- **Action:** Reflect on moments in the past week when you felt overwhelmed, rushed, or anxious.
- **Ask Yourself:**
- When did I feel agitated or restless?
- Was I trying to accomplish too much at once, or feeling dissatisfied

with what I had achieved?

- **Write down** 3 specific situations from the past week when you noticed Rajas affecting your energy or mindset.

Examples:

- *I felt rushed all day, trying to finish multiple tasks at once, and ended up feeling anxious and unproductive.*
- *I couldn't focus on one thing for too long, jumping from task to task without finishing any of them.*
- *I kept thinking about future plans and felt restless about not being where I wanted to be in life.*

3. Recognize the Effects of Rajas on Your Mental and Emotional State

- **Action:** Observe how Rajas affects your physical, mental, and emotional well-being. Recognize how agitation and overactivity may drain your energy and create anxiety.
- **Ask Yourself:**
- How do I feel physically and mentally when I am caught up in the restlessness of Rajas?
- How does Rajas impact my emotional balance and my relationships with others?
- **Write down** your observations about how Rajas influences your mental and emotional state.

Examples:

- *When I'm caught up in Rajas, I feel mentally scattered, stressed, and physically tense.*

- *My emotions become erratic, and I have trouble finding peace, which affects my relationships and decision-making.*
- *Rajas causes me to lose focus and makes everything feel urgent, even when it isn't.*

4. Cultivate Calmness and Focus to Balance Rajas

- **Action:** Today, set an intention to bring calmness, balance, and focus to your actions by moderating your activities and reducing overexertion.
- **Ask Yourself:**
- What activities can I engage in today that help me slow down and find inner peace?
- How can I be more mindful and focused in my actions rather than feeling driven by constant restlessness?
- **Write down** actions you will take today to counterbalance Rajas and promote calmness.

Examples:

- *I will practice taking short breaks between tasks to avoid burnout and calm my mind.*
- *I will focus on one task at a time, bringing my full attention to it instead of multitasking.*
- *I will spend a few minutes in meditation or deep breathing to help ground my energy.*

5. Observe Shifts in Energy and Calmness

- **Action:** For the next 12 hours, observe your energy levels, mental clarity, and emotional balance as you practice moderation and calmness.
- **Ask Yourself:**
- How does my energy shift when I consciously slow down and focus on the present moment?
- Do I feel more peaceful and less restless after reducing overactivity?
- **Write down** your observations about how moderating Rajas has affected your state of being.

Examples:

- *After focusing on one task, I felt more productive and less overwhelmed by everything on my to-do list.*
- *When I took breaks, I noticed that I felt more relaxed and clear-headed, as opposed to constantly running on stress.*
- *I felt more at peace when I stopped thinking about the future and just focused on what was happening now.*

6. Evening Reflection (Journaling)

- **Action:** Before ending your day, reflect on your experience of moderating Rajas and balancing your energy. Here are some guiding questions to help you structure your journaling:
- How did I feel when I noticed Rajas affecting my actions and energy today?
- *Example: I realized how anxious I was about my to-do list, and how it affected my mood and focus.*
- What steps did I take to reduce overactivity and restlessness, and how did they help?

- *Example: I consciously took breaks and worked in smaller, focused chunks of time. This helped me calm down and feel more productive.*
- How did I feel after slowing down and balancing my energy?
- *Example: I felt less stressed, and my mind was clearer when I focused on one thing at a time.*
- What have I learned about managing restlessness and balancing Rajas in my life?
- *Example: I learned that slowing down and focusing on the present moment helps reduce my anxiety and overactivity.*

Guided by Bhagavad Gita Wisdom

Rajas is the quality of activity, restlessness, and attachment. As Krishna explains in Chapter 14, Verse 7:

"Know Rajas to be born of desire, O Arjuna; it binds the embodied soul by attachment, passion, and restless activity."

Krishna teaches that by moderating Rajas through discipline, mindfulness, and self-awareness, we can attain inner balance and peace. By bringing awareness to our energy and actions, we reduce distractions and focus on spiritual growth rather than being overwhelmed by external desires.

Relevance

Moderating Rajas helps us cultivate calmness, clarity, and steady focus, enabling us to engage in purposeful action, reduce anxiety, and strengthen our spiritual practice.

End of Day 19

Summary:

- Today, you identified how Rajas (overactivity and restlessness) can negatively affect your energy and mental state.

- You practiced balancing this energy by slowing down, focusing on one task at a time, and cultivating calmness.
- Moderating Rajas helps you find peace, clarity, and emotional balance, allowing you to function more effectively in all areas of life.

21

Day 20: Cultivating Sattva (Purity, Harmony, and Lightness)

Purpose: To cultivate Sattva, the quality of purity, harmony, and lightness, which promotes mental clarity, balance, and spiritual growth, leading to peace and contentment.

Vaidehi and the Classroom Symphony

Vaidehi loved teaching, but recently she felt like her classroom had turned into chaos—not just with her students, but inside her own mind. Papers piled up, deadlines loomed, and small frustrations—like a student shouting across the room or a forgotten homework—made her chest tighten. Even her favorite part of the day, reading stories to her students, felt heavy and rushed.

One afternoon, while rearranging her classroom, she found a small, dusty music box that belonged to her grandmother. Curiously, she wound it up. As the soft, delicate tune filled the room, something unusual happened. Her students fell silent, drawn to the gentle sound. The noise of pencils dropping, chairs scraping, and whispered chatter seemed to fade. Vaidehi felt herself breathe more deeply; her mind uncluttered, her heart lighter.

In that moment, she realized she had glimpsed Sattva—pure, harmonious, light energy. It wasn't just about a tidy classroom or a quiet moment; it was about how she approached everything: her thoughts, her actions, and her presence. She understood that cultivating Sattva meant noticing the small beauties in life, staying calm amidst activity, and acting with clarity and intention rather than reaction.

From that day onward, Vaidehi began small, intentional practices. She started each morning with a brief mindfulness ritual, feeling the rhythm of her breath before the students arrived. She organized her lessons with a sense of calm, rather than rushing, and even found moments of creative play—letting students illustrate stories instead of racing through them. When challenges arose, she paused, took a breath, and responded with balance and clarity. Even in hectic moments, she felt a sense of inner lightness that had been missing before.

By evening, Vaidehi noticed how different she felt. Her mind was clear, her interactions warm, and her heart peaceful. Sattva wasn't a distant ideal—it was a living, breathing quality she could invite into every moment with intention.

As she journaled that night, she wrote:

"Today I discovered that harmony and lightness are never far away. By slowing down, observing, and approaching each moment with care, my mind feels lighter, my heart more open, and my day more joyful."

Like Vaidehi, we all have moments where life feels heavy or chaotic. The practice of Sattva invites us to pause, find inner clarity, and approach each moment with purity, harmony, and lightness.

1. Understand the Concept of Sattva (Purity, Harmony, and Lightness)

- **Action:** Reflect on the qualities of Sattva—purity, mental clarity, harmony, and balance. Sattva brings peace to the mind and body, enabling a deeper connection to your higher self.
- **Simple Explanation:** Sattva is the quality of goodness, light, and clarity. It is the foundation of spiritual growth, as it allows one to connect with their true self and experience a peaceful state of being.
- **Example:***When I feel calm, content, and mentally clear, that is Sattva within me. I feel peaceful and aligned with my highest values.*

2. Identify Moments of Sattva in Your Life

- **Action:** Reflect on moments in the past week when you experienced purity, clarity, peace, and balance in your thoughts and actions.

- **Ask Yourself:**
- When did I feel a sense of calm and clarity?
- What activities or experiences brought harmony and peace to my mind?
- **Write down** 3 specific situations from the past week when you noticed the presence of Sattva in your thoughts, feelings, or actions.

Examples:

- *During my meditation, I felt a deep sense of inner peace and clarity, which stayed with me throughout the day.*
- *When I spent time in nature, I felt connected to something larger than myself, and I experienced a sense of harmony and lightness.*
- *I felt at ease and centered during a challenging conversation, choosing to respond with kindness and patience instead of reacting.*

3. Recognize the Effects of Sattva on Your Mental and Emotional State

- **Action:** Observe how Sattva affects your physical, mental, and emotional well-being. Recognize how purity and clarity bring a sense of lightness, joy, and inner peace.
- **Ask Yourself:**
- How do I feel physically and mentally when I am experiencing the effects of Sattva?
- How does Sattva influence my emotional balance and relationships with others?
- **Write down** your observations about how Sattva influences your mental and emotional state.

Examples:

- *When I feel the presence of Sattva, my mind is calm, and I am able to think clearly and make decisions from a place of wisdom.*
- *Sattva helps me feel balanced and in harmony, which strengthens my relationships and ability to respond to others with empathy.*
- *Physically, I feel lighter and more energized when I am aligned with Sattva, and my body feels less tense or fatigued.*

4. Cultivate Sattva Through Daily Practices

- **Action:** Today, set an intention to cultivate Sattva in your life through practices that promote purity, mental clarity, and harmony.
- **Ask Yourself:**
- What activities or habits can I engage in to invite more Sattva into my life?
- How can I ensure that my thoughts, actions, and relationships align with the qualities of purity, peace, and balance?
- **Write down** actions you will take today to cultivate Sattva and bring more harmony into your life.

Examples:

- *I will practice mindfulness throughout the day, focusing on my breath and the present moment to cultivate peace and clarity.*
- *I will engage in a creative activity, such as painting or writing, to express my inner purity and connect with my higher self.*
- *I will consciously choose to speak kindly and act with compassion, aiming to create harmony in my interactions.*

5. Observe the Shifts in Your Energy and Mindset

- **Action:** For the next 12 hours, observe your energy levels, mental clarity, and emotional state as you focus on cultivating Sattva.
- **Ask Yourself:**
- How does my energy feel when I consciously nurture Sattva?
- Do I feel more at peace, focused, and balanced as I invite more purity and harmony into my life?
- **Write down** your observations about how Sattva affects your state of being throughout the day.

Examples:

- *As I focused on being mindful and present, I felt a sense of calm that allowed me to be more productive and focused.*
- *The peace I experienced during my meditation carried over into my interactions, and I was able to remain patient and centered.*
- *I felt lighter and more joyful when I spent time in activities that nurtured my inner purity, like reading or being in nature.*

6. Evening Reflection (Journaling)

- **Action:** Before ending your day, reflect on your experience of cultivating Sattva and balancing your energy. Here are some guiding questions to help you structure your journaling:
- How did I feel when I consciously cultivated Sattva today?
- *Example: I felt more peaceful and balanced, and my mind was clearer throughout the day.*
- What practices or actions helped me align with the qualities of Sattva?

- *Example: I felt grounded and centered after meditating and focusing on my breath.*
- How did I notice the presence of Sattva in my relationships and actions today?
- *Example: I was more patient and kind in my conversations, which deepened my connection with others.*
- How can I bring more of Sattva into my daily life moving forward?
- *Example: I will continue to set aside time for quiet reflection and mindfulness to nurture peace and clarity.*

Guided by Bhagavad Gita Wisdom

Sattva is the quality of purity, harmony, and lightness. As Krishna explains in Chapter 14, Verse 6:

"Know Sattva to be born of wisdom, O Arjuna; it illuminates the mind and binds the embodied soul by purity, knowledge, and happiness."

Krishna teaches that by cultivating Sattva, we experience mental clarity, inner peace, and spiritual fulfillment. Sattva aligns our thoughts, actions, and relationships with wisdom and harmony, leading to a deeper connection with the divine and higher consciousness.

Relevance

Cultivating Sattva helps purify the mind and heart, fosters clarity, balance, and joy, and strengthens spiritual awareness. By nurturing this quality, we can act with kindness, peace, and wisdom in all aspects of life.

End of Day 20

Summary:

- Today, you focused on cultivating Sattva, the quality of purity, mental clarity, and harmony.

- By nurturing Sattva, you experienced a deeper connection with your inner peace and joy.
- Moving forward, you can continue to bring Sattva into your life through mindfulness, self-reflection, and acts of kindness, creating a more balanced and harmonious state of being.

22

Day 21: Final Reflection: Integrating Lessons and Next Steps

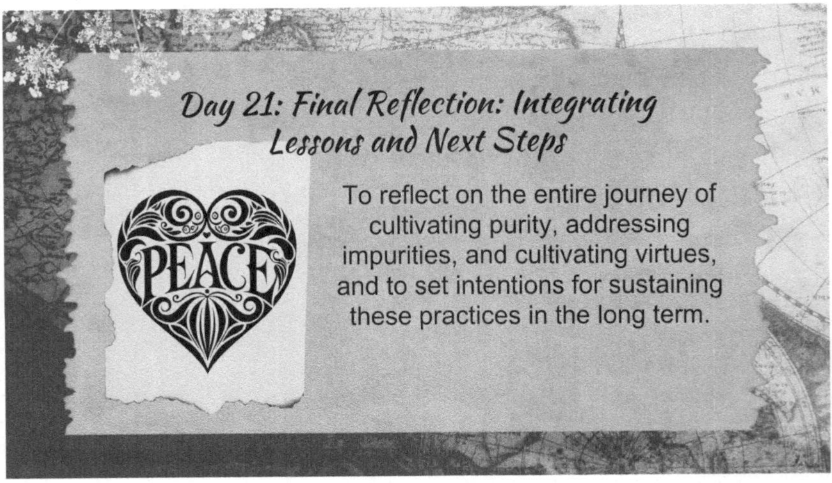

Purpose: To reflect on the entire journey of cultivating purity, addressing impurities, and cultivating virtues, and to set intentions for sustaining these practices in the long term.

Aarushi and the Garden of Reflections

Aarushi had spent the last three weeks deeply immersed in a journey of self-discovery. As an architect, she was used to designing buildings—carefully placing each element to create harmony and balance—but she realized that she had never paid the same attention to designing her inner life. Her thoughts, reactions, and emotions often felt scattered, like unfinished blueprints in her mind.

On this final day, Aarushi decided to take a walk in the small garden behind her home, a place she often ignored in her busy schedule. As she wandered among the flowering plants, listening to the rustle of leaves and the hum of bees, she noticed something subtle: every plant, every petal, every tiny movement in nature seemed perfectly in its place, balanced and alive. A quiet thought arose in her: *If nature can maintain such harmony effortlessly, can I learn to do the same within myself?*

Aarushi sat on a bench and reflected on the past 21 days. She remembered moments when she had been quick to anger or impatient with colleagues, moments when her desires had made her restless, and moments when she had felt disconnected from her own inner light. But she also remembered the small victories: the times she had paused before reacting, the moments of gratitude that shifted her perspective, and the mindfulness practices that brought clarity to her mind.

She realized that, like tending a garden, cultivating virtues required patience, care, and consistent attention. Weeds of pride, envy, or greed might still appear, but with awareness and gentle effort, they could be removed, making room for flowers of compassion, calmness, and clarity to grow.

By evening, Aarushi felt a deep sense of integration. She made a few notes in her journal:

"I see how far I've come—not in perfection, but in awareness and intention. I am learning to nurture my mind and heart, just like a garden. Each day is an opportunity to continue growing, to respond with patience, and to live with clarity and harmony."

Aarushi's next steps were clear: she would continue her daily meditation, remain mindful of her reactions, practice gratitude, and keep observing her thoughts with gentle curiosity. The journey wasn't ending; it was transforming into a lifelong practice of self-reflection, surrender, and growth.

Like Aarushi, we all reach moments where reflection helps us see the bigger picture. The final day invites us to integrate the lessons, acknowledge our growth, and set intentions for the continued journey of cultivating virtues, surrendering the ego, and living with inner harmony.

1. Reflect on Your Journey

- **Action:** Take a moment to reflect on the entire process of the past three weeks, from recognizing and addressing impurities to cultivating virtues that replace them. Consider your growth, challenges, and moments of insight.
- **Ask Yourself:**
- How have I grown in the past three weeks in terms of my thoughts, actions, and emotional responses?
- What have been the key shifts in my mindset and behavior?
- **Write down** your reflections on how you've changed over the last three weeks.

Examples:

- *I feel like I've developed a stronger awareness of my emotions, especially anger and greed, and I've learned how to shift them toward patience and contentment.*
- *I have noticed that I feel calmer and more focused, and I'm able to respond with greater empathy and compassion instead of reacting impulsively.*
- *I now understand the importance of self-discipline in achieving detachment from desires, and I feel more balanced and grounded.*

2. Review Specific Moments of Growth

- **Action:** Revisit the key moments of growth and transformation over the past three weeks. Identify specific actions or experiences that represent your progress and the changes you've made.
- **Ask Yourself:**
- What were the most significant moments of growth during this journey?
- What actions or reflections were particularly helpful in shifting my mindset or behavior?
- **Write down** 3 significant moments that represent your growth.

Examples:

- *The moment I chose to respond with compassion during a difficult conversation instead of anger was a key breakthrough.*
- *Realizing how practicing gratitude shifted my perspective from scarcity to abundance helped me overcome feelings of greed.*
- *During my meditation, I was able to clearly see how my attachment to*

outcomes had been clouding my peace, and I started letting go.

3. Assess Current Impurities and Virtues

- **Action:** Reflect on your current state. What are the impurities that still need attention? Which virtues are beginning to take root in your life?
- **Ask Yourself:**
- Which impurities (pride, envy, anger, greed, etc.) do I still notice in my life?
- Which virtues have become more prominent or natural for me over the past few weeks?
- **Write down** the impurities that still need attention and the virtues that are now more prominent in your life.

Examples:

- *I still notice moments of comparison and envy when I see others succeeding, but I've become more aware of it and am working on cultivating compassion.*
- *Humility and forgiveness have become more natural for me, especially in situations where I might have reacted defensively before.*

4. Plan for Sustaining Growth

- **Action:** Set intentions for how you will continue to cultivate and integrate these lessons moving forward. What daily or weekly practices can you commit to?
- **Ask Yourself:**

- How can I continue to practice and strengthen the virtues I've cultivated over the past three weeks?
- What steps can I take to ensure that I don't fall back into old patterns?
- **Write down** a few actionable steps or daily practices that will help you sustain your growth.

Examples:

- *I will dedicate 10 minutes each morning to meditation and self-reflection to maintain clarity and focus.*
- *I will consciously practice gratitude every evening before bed, noting three things I'm grateful for.*
- *I will be more mindful of my reactions and choose compassion when I feel triggered by pride or anger.*

5. Set Your Next Steps for Spiritual and Personal Growth

- **Action:** Think about your next steps in this journey of self-development. What further spiritual practices, virtues, or goals would you like to pursue?
- **Ask Yourself:**
- What are my next spiritual or personal growth goals after this 21-day journey?
- How can I continue to build on what I've learned?
- **Write down** your next steps, goals, or areas of focus for further growth.

Examples:

- *I will dive deeper into the practice of detachment, learning how to surrender to the flow of life more fully.*
- *I want to focus on cultivating more patience and resilience in challenging situations.*
- *I will continue to explore timeless wisdom and apply its teachings to all areas of my life, deepening my connection with the divine.*

6. Evening Reflection (Journaling)

- **Action:** Before ending your day, reflect on the entire process and any insights you've gained in this final reflection.
- **Ask Yourself:**
- How do I feel as I conclude this 21-day journey?
- What lessons have I learned, and how can I continue applying them?
- **Write down** your reflections on the entire 21-day journey.

Examples:

- *This journey has given me more clarity and peace than I expected. I feel more connected to my higher self and less caught up in ego and distractions.*
- *I have learned the importance of self-reflection and making small, conscious choices every day to shift my mindset and emotions.*
- *I feel empowered to continue this practice and deepen my spiritual growth as I move forward.*

Guided by Bhagavad Gita Wisdom

Krishna emphasizes the ultimate importance of surrender in Chapter 18, Verse 66:

"Abandon all varieties of dharma and simply surrender unto Me alone. I will liberate you from all sinful reactions; do not fear."

This teaching highlights that after cultivating virtues, reducing impurities, and integrating self-discipline, the final step is surrendering the ego and all actions to the divine. By letting go of personal attachment and fully relying on Krishna's guidance, we align with our highest self and move toward liberation.

Relevance

Surrendering the ego and integrating the lessons of the 21-day journey allows us to embody spiritual wisdom in daily life. It fosters inner peace, clarity, devotion, and the ability to act with humility, ensuring that our growth continues beyond structured practice into a lifelong path of self-realization and spiritual alignment.

End of Day 21

Summary:

- Today, you reflected on your journey of cultivating virtues and overcoming impurities. You recognized the growth you've experienced and set intentions for sustaining this positive transformation in the future.
- Moving forward, continue to practice the lessons you've learned and stay committed to your path of growth and spiritual development.

23

Glossary

Aarav / Avantika / Vaidehi / Neel / Sameer / Aarushi etc – Characters used throughout the 21-day journey to illustrate real-life applications of spiritual principles. They symbolize common human experiences with desires, emotions, and growth.

Abhyasa – Practice or consistent effort; spiritual discipline through repeated practice.

Anger (Krodha) – Emotional reaction arising from frustration or unmet desires. Recognized as a key impurity to overcome through patience, reflection, and self-control.

Atma-Vidya – Self-knowledge; awareness of one's true spiritual nature beyond ego and physical identity.

Bhagavad Gita – Ancient Indian scripture that provides guidance on life, dharma (duty), self-realization, and spiritual wisdom.

Devotion (Bhakti) – Loving dedication and surrender to the divine, considered a path to purify the heart and mind.

Dharma – Righteous duty or life purpose; acting in alignment with moral, ethical, and spiritual principles.

Detachment (Vairagya) – Letting go of excessive attachment to material outcomes, relationships, or personal ego.

Ego – The sense of individual identity and self-importance that can create separation from spiritual awareness.

Envy (Matsarya) – Resentment or desire arising from comparison with others; recognized as an impurity to overcome.

Gratitude (Santosh) – Recognizing and appreciating divine grace and the blessings in life; fosters positivity and purification of mind.

Impurities / Inner Challenges – Negative qualities such as lust, anger, greed, pride, envy, and delusion that cloud the mind and obstruct spiritual growth.

Inertia / Tamas – The quality of heaviness, ignorance, or lethargy in the mind and body that reduces clarity, motivation, and awareness (Bhagavad Gita 14.8).

Joy / Bliss (Ananda) – Natural state of contentment and peace arising when the mind is purified and aligned with spiritual truth.

Karma – Actions and their consequences; performing duties mindfully and selflessly is emphasized in the Gita.

Lust / Desire (Kama) – Excessive craving or attachment to sensory pleasures, relationships, or outcomes; overcome through selfless love and detachment.

Moderation / Balance – Harmonizing physical, mental, and emotional energies; regulating activity to prevent restlessness (Rajas) or inertia (Tamas).

Patience / Titiksha – The ability to endure difficulties and delay gratification without agitation; linked to overcoming anger and restlessness.

Pride / Ahankar – Ego-driven self-importance or arrogance; a key impurity addressed in the journey.

Purity / Sattva – Quality of lightness, clarity, harmony, and goodness; fosters mental clarity, peace, and spiritual growth (Bhagavad Gita 14.6).

Rajas – The quality of activity, restlessness, and desire-driven energy that can lead to anxiety and distraction if unbalanced (Bhagavad Gita 14.7).

Resilience – Capacity to recover from challenges, maintain emotional stability, and persevere with a steady mind.

Selfless Action / Nishkam Karma – Performing duties without attachment to the results, aligning actions with dharma and divine guidance.

Self-Discipline (Abhyasa / Tapas) – Consistent effort to regulate mind, body, and habits; key to overcoming impurities.

Surrender (Sharanagati) – Relinquishing ego, desires, and control to the divine, trusting in divine wisdom and guidance (Bhagavad Gita 18.66).

Virtues / Qualities to Cultivate – Positive traits such as compassion, empathy, kindness, patience, clarity, humility, mindfulness, and contentment that counteract impurities.

Wisdom (Jnana / Viveka) – Discernment, self-knowledge, and insight into right action and spiritual truth.

24

Conclusion

Celebrating the Journey

Congratulations on completing the 21-Day Emotional and Spiritual Detox!

Today marks the beautiful culmination of this transformative journey, and it is time to honor **YOU**—your commitment, dedication, and courage in embracing this powerful process of self-growth.

This book has been more than a 21-day guide; it has been an invitation to reconnect with your true self, to shed old layers, and to step into your highest potential. By consciously detoxing emotionally and spiritually, you've created space for a new version of yourself—one that is aligned with purity, compassion, and inner peace.

Let's Celebrate Your Transformation

Throughout these pages, you've met Aarav, Meera, Anika, Rohan, Vikram, Tara, Nisha, Arjun, Priya, Vaidehi, and Neel—each navigating their own path of reflection, learning, and growth. Their stories are mirrors of your own journey. Just as they discovered new clarity, harmony, and strength, you too have taken steps toward cultivating virtues and releasing patterns that no longer serve you.

Pause for a moment and celebrate everything you've achieved:

- You've gained clarity by reflecting on your emotions and thoughts.
- You've cultivated virtues that support your spiritual and emotional growth.
- You've released old patterns and created space for new energy.
- You've strengthened your connection to your inner self and your higher consciousness.

Take a deep breath. Give yourself a pat on the back. Feel the gratitude for the courage it took to embark on this journey and the dedication you have shown every day.

What's Next?

Although this 21-day journey concludes here, your path of self-development continues. Carry the lessons, tools, and wisdom you've gathered into every day of your life.

- Continue practicing the virtues you've nurtured.
- Sustain your growth through reflection, mindfulness, and devotion.
- Lead your life with compassion, clarity, and presence.

Just as Aarav, Meera, Anika, Rohan, Vikram, Tara, Nisha, Arjun, Priya, Vaidehi, and Neel have walked their paths in these stories, **your transformation is ongoing**—one conscious choice at a time.

"This journey is yours. Celebrate it. Live it. And let the growth continue every day."

Epilogue

You have completed your 21-day journey. You have observed how lust, anger, greed, pride, envy, and delusion appear in your life, and you have practiced letting go, reflecting, and cultivating virtues like love, humility, and contentment.

This journey is ongoing. The awareness, reflections, and exercises you've practiced are tools you can return to whenever life feels overwhelming, unclear, or challenging.

Through Aarav's story, the experiences of workshop participants, and Krishna's timeless guidance, may you continue toward **clarity, peace, and spiritual alignment**. Every day is an opportunity to grow and live purposefully.

Afterword

This book bridges the **timeless teachings of the Bhagavad Gita** with real human experience. The 21-day program is a practical guide to recognizing and overcoming the inner impurities that disturb peace and clarity.

Use this book as a companion whenever you need to:

- Observe your thoughts and emotions without judgment.
- Recognize attachments and tendencies that disturb your inner balance.
- Apply practical exercises to cultivate peace, self-awareness, and emotional resilience.
- Revisit the wisdom of Krishna for guidance, reflection, and clarity.

May this journey empower you to live with a **calm mind, a pure heart, and aligned purpose**.

About the Author

About the Author

Vijayshree Ratanparkhe has long been guided by the timeless wisdom of the Bhagavad Gita, which she has studied, reflected upon, and lived through her own experiences. Her spiritual journey has been one of self-discovery, discipline, and mindful transformation, learning to navigate the challenges of the mind, emotions, and everyday life with clarity and balance.

Through her work, Vijayshree seeks to translate the profound teachings of the Gita into practical guidance for modern readers, helping them overcome inner challenges such as anger, greed, envy, pride, lust, and restlessness, and cultivate virtues like patience, clarity, compassion, and self-awareness. Her writing emphasizes that spiritual growth is a daily practice—a journey of small, intentional steps toward inner harmony, balance, and peace.

This 21-day program reflects her commitment to making spiritual principles accessible and actionable, showing readers how to integrate the Gita's teachings into their personal and emotional lives. Vijayshree's gentle guidance inspires readers to observe, reflect, and transform, cultivating a life of purpose, clarity, and inner light.

You can connect with me on:
- https://shreesessencia.com
- https://x.com/Vijayshreerp
- https://www.facebook.com/shreesessencia
- https://www.linkedin.com/in/vijayshree-r-48024aa6

Also by Vijayshree R

Vijayshree Ratanparkhe is a spiritual guide, author, and workshop facilitator whose work bridges the timeless wisdom of the Bhagavad Gita with practical guidance for personal growth, emotional well-being, and purposeful living. Her writing focuses on **transforming human experiences into actionable insights**, helping readers recognize their inner challenges, awaken self-awareness, and live a life of clarity, balance, and fulfillment.

Through her work, Vijayshree helps readers turn challenges into opportunities for growth, offering tools and inspiration to live a life aligned with spiritual principles and practical wisdom.

Avantika's Train to Truth – The Journey to Your Life's Purpose

Life's journey is rarely a straight track—it bends, halts, and challenges us to choose who we will become. In Avantika's Train to Truth, a young woman faces obstacles that force her to question everything she knows. With courage as her ticket and the Bhagavad Gita as her compass, she learns how to turn doubt into direction and struggle into purpose. Inspiring and deeply relatable, this story invites every reader to board their own train toward truth, clarity, and fulfillment.

When Children Forget, Life Remembers

Every parent gives everything to their children—but what remains when the nest empties and love seems forgotten? When Children Forget, Life Remembers traces Jagdish and Lalitha's journey from heartbreak to healing. With the Bhagavad Gita as their compass, they discover that emptiness is not an ending, but an invitation to deeper love and higher purpose. Gentle, wise, and universal, this story reminds us that love rooted in the soul never disappears—it only changes form.

Printed at Repro India Ltd.